W9-ATR-474

WHY AM I DOING THIS?

Contributing Authors

Julie Amodeo

Jill Berkowicz

Rebecca Collins

Diane Cunningham

Robin Grusko

Elizabeth Locatelli

Marcia Lubell

Bill Peppiatt

Robin Sostak

WHY AM I DOING THIS?
Purposeful Teaching Through Portfolio Assessment

Giselle O. Martin-Kniep

with
Diane Cunningham, Diana Muxworthy Feige,
and the Teachers from the Hudson Valley
Portfolio Assessment Project

HEINEMANN
Portsmouth, NH

Heinemann
A division of Reed Elsevier Inc.
361 Hanover Street
Portsmouth, NH 03801–3912

Offices and agents throughout the world

© 1998 by Giselle O. Martin-Kniep

All rights reserved. No part of this book may be reproduced in any form or by any electronic or mechanical means, including information storage and retrieval systems, without permission in writing from the publisher, except by a reviewer, who may quote brief passages in a review.

Library of Congress Cataloging-in-Publication Data
Martin-Kniep, Giselle O.
   Why am I doing this? : purposeful teaching through portfolio assessment / by Giselle O. Martin-Kniep, with Diane Cunningham, Diana Muxworthy Feige, and teachers from the Hudson Valley Portfolio Assessment Project.
      p.   cm.
   Includes index.
   ISBN 0-325-00010-7
   1. Hudson Valley Portfolio Assessment Project.   2. Portfolios in education—New York (State)   3. Educational tests and measurements—New York (State)   I. Cunningham, Diane. II. Feige, Diana Muxworthy.   III. Hudson Valley Portfolio Assessment Project.   IV. Title.
   LB1029.P67M37   1998
   371.27—dc21   97-51793
                                                                                              CIP

Production: Abigail M. Heim
Cover design: Darci Mehall, Aureo Design
Manufacturing: Louise Richardson

Printed in the United States of America on acid-free paper

02   01   00   99   98   ML   2   3   4   5

371.27
M38

99-0228
38126013

Contents

Acknowledgments

The Hudson Valley Portfolio Assessment Project (HVPAP) was a product of collective faith and commitment. It would have never been possible without the enthusiasm and trust of the six individuals who actively negotiated its existence. These individuals, each of whom represented a different regional Board of Cooperative Educational Services (BOCES), are Leslie Anderson, Nancy Anderson, Jane Bullowa, Joe Gibson, Wayne Mengel, and Candace Mazur. The initiative became a laboratory of good practice, providing a forum for the discussion of essential educational questions through the active participation of many teachers and administrators who became and/or supported the Hudson Valley faculty. This group taught me more about the possibilities of education than I ever thought possible.

I would have never been able to provide all the support that participants needed in this project on my own. Our support team, comprised of my friends and colleagues Diane Cunningham, Margot Dieckmann, Diana Muxworthy Feige, Suzi Grodin, and Devin Thornburg, was instrumental to the success of the project. I thank Grant Wiggins for planting the seeds and raising the questions.

This book has been the culmination of a dream to develop a professional piece of work produced by teachers, university faculty, and professional developers. The teachers who wrote their stories—Julie Amodeo, Jill Berkowicz, Rebecca Collins, Robin Grusko, Liz Locatelli, Marcia Lubell, Bill Peppiatt, and Robin Sostak—embody the qualities of exemplary practice and will never cease to inspire me. Their voices, as well as mine, were unified and clarified through the craftsmanship and talent of Diane Cunningham and Diana Muxworthy Feige, my two friends and editors.

On a more personal note, I want to thank my daughter Liah for teaching me about what youngsters need from schools and for inspiring me to do this work.

Sponsoring BOCES and HVPAP Participants

Dutchess County BOCES

Margaret Brizzie
Bruce Cohen
Michael Foley
Susan J. Franke
Pamela Gatje
Kathy Griffin
Anne E. Halstead
Michael McCormack
Wayne Mengel
Vincent Nugent
Erin O'Neill
Pattie Sherman
Sally W. Sober
Rosemarie Stark
Fran Todd
Andy Verdon
Lynda Vincent

Orange Ulster BOCES

Julie Amodeo
Nancy Anderson
Kathryn M. Bauer
Carolyn Bender
Joseph Carillo
Larry Diulio
Jennifer C. Hammond-King
Mary Ann Heaney
James Hyland
Wayne Mengel
Iris Mitzner
Carol Napolitano
Patricia Papini
Lorraine Perrego
Jayne Peterson
Nancy Prather
Elisa Roman
Roslyn Rubenstein
Mary Ellen Schmick
Evelyn Schneider

Janet L. Seaman
Dina Shortall
Cynthia Vanchy
Wendi Zecher

Putnam/Northern Westchester County BOCES

Cherie Amdur
Joanne Anderson
Leslie Anderson
Rebecca Collins
Elizabeth N. Flor
Karyn Ganz-Moro
Marla Gardner
Joanne Gibbs
Robin Grusko
Loretta Hirschmugl
Lorraine Isaac
Norma Johnson
Tom Kersting
Sally Kuralt
Robyn Lane
Jane Lemak
Marcia Lubell
Lori Ann Perrelle
James Quinn
Joan Schlosser
Paul J. Smith
Allan Wallowitz
Pat Wistort
Douglas Young

Rockland County BOCES

Mary Affronti
Robert Colombo
Diane Courtney
Elizabeth Danahy
Diane Gasparrini
Eileen Gehsman
Joe Gibson

Nancy Goldman
Judy Goldstein
Wendy Gottleib
Lynda Hammond
Karen Hofstetter
Joan Hutton
Connie Jaworski
Eileen Lennon
Liz Locatelli
Helen Lynch
Florence Manoff
Carol Martin
Lisa Monte
Maureen O'Connor
William Peppiatt
Beth Poidevin
Eileen Porcu
Robin Rogers
Ray Roswell
Rhoda Schaefer
Joseph Sciortino
Ann Singer
Judith Tamsky
Audrey Verboys
Harriet Yustein

David Lubin
Candace Mazur
Mary Ann Mullen
Dorothy Novogrodsky
Joan Skalsky
Robin Sostak
Marilyn J. Sperber
Dorothy VanLoon

Ulster County BOCES

Carolyn Bagley
Beth Barlow
Mary Ann Bruck
Jane Bullowa
Lisa Congers
Marney L. Janson
Dawn Krom
Carolyn Kuhlmann
Carol LaMonda
Debra Lundgren
Helen Tennenbaum
Barbara Vetucci
Dennis Warner
Susan Waters

Sullivan County BOCES

Jill Berkowicz
Neil Bright
Regina Campbell
Debbie Dunwell
Constance H. Elberth
Deborah Glatt

WHY AM I DOING THIS?

Introduction
Giselle O. Martin-Kniep

Teachers must have access to professional development models that
recognize what teachers know, are respectful of teachers' learning
process, and enable them to see themselves as learners who are
responsible for their own profession.

Giselle O. Martin-Kniep

*Giselle Martin-Kniep is the President of Learner-Centered Initiatives,
Ltd., an educational consulting organization specializing in regional
and school-based curriculum and assessment initiatives. She has a
strong background in organizational change, a doctorate in social
sciences in Education, and a Ed.S. degree in educational evaluation.
From 1990 to 1995 she was a faculty member in the School
of Education at Adelphi University. She has served as a program
evaluator, researcher, and curriculum developer. In the last eight
years, she has worked with numerous schools and districts
in the areas of alternative assessment, curriculum design,
school change, and teacher research. She has designed
and directed five comprehensive, multiyear, regional
and school-based professional development programs in the
United States aimed at transforming curriculum and assessment
practices among K–12 teachers. Together, these projects have
involved more than 500 teachers from over 75 school districts.*

Teaching is like no other profession. At the very least, it involves a constant
translation between what a teacher knows and what students are yet to discover or confirm. At its best, it is a performance of inspiration and elegance.
Teachers understand aspects of children's learning that are obscure to most
people, and, like the Inuits' recognition of many different kinds of snow,
teachers can identify the subtleties of learning in multiple shades of grey.

We, as a society, do not act as if we believe in this professionalism. We
treat teachers as custodians, as implementers of other people's knowledge,

and as the technicians of that factory we call school. How else could we explain our endorsement of schedules that require elementary school teachers to deal with the disruptions associated with multiple pullouts, or with the reality of five or six preparation periods or of thirty-minute lunch breaks at 10:30 A.M.? Our staff development models, as well, reflect this lack of understanding and respect for the intricacies of the teaching endeavor. We expect teachers, for example, to attend one or two conferences on the latest technology and then implement it comprehensively in their classrooms. We also tend to assume that outside consultants, and not teachers, are best equipped to provide teachers with needed knowledge and skills.

Ironically, I am one of those outside consultants—a consultant and staff developer who believes that teacher learning can be maximized under certain conditions. Some of these conditions include having teachers study their practice through action research and teacher inquiry; inviting teachers to work collaboratively, instead of experiencing new learning as individuals isolated from their peers; developing programs that balance in-depth exposure to learning situations with opportunities to apply such learning in their own classrooms; and combining the teaching of content knowledge with learning about how best to teach it.

I came to embrace these beliefs when I worked as a researcher, curriculum developer, and program evaluator at Stanford University, where I also completed my graduate and postgraduate studies. As a researcher working on a three-year longitudinal study on individual and organizational factors that support teacher change, I learned that change in practice can only happen under specific circumstances. As a curriculum developer, I learned that teachers seldom can or are asked to develop the curriculum they teach, relying instead on "experts" who are more interested in content and skill acquisition than in addressing the contexts for teaching and learning. As a program evaluator, I learned that many staff development opportunities for teachers lack the rigor and follow-through that is necessary to support desired changes, and that there is often a mismatch between teachers' needs and work conditions and the staff development goals.

It is fair to say that my experiences at Stanford and in California provided me with a strong foundation for developing the approaches to professional development that have framed my work in New York and in other states. They have also allowed me to recognize—and be awed by—teachers' unique knowledge base. Teacher expertise is as rich in its forms and nuances as other kinds of professional expertise. It becomes apparent, though, in the seemingly effortless dance between a teacher and her students as they engage in powerful learning activities; in the delicate interplay of the classroom give-and-take that occurs throughout the day, closely mirroring what most international negotiators practice all their lives for; and in the spontaneity with which teachers can transform what appear to be digressions into timely, teachable moments.

As the director of the Hudson Valley Portfolio Assessment Project, I yearned for a community of learners that allowed teachers to recognize, articulate, and communicate their professional knowledge. I wanted to help provide the structures and language for teachers to articulate their own professionalism. I wanted to use the exploration of assessment as a vehicle for teachers to question their own knowledge and skills, and, in so doing, find the essence of what drives them as teachers. I hoped that through a sustained process of inquiry, reflection, and communication, teachers would become avid learners of their own expertise.

Over the course of the past three years, I have found support for my beliefs in teachers' professional knowledge base. The value of teachers' self-discovery as learners is also evident in the changing roles that many of the project participants have assumed. This book tells the story of our collective transformation.

This book is divided into three parts. The first one includes three chapters that describe the history, underlying assumptions, and program components of the Hudson Valley Portfolio Assessment Project. The second part includes eight stories of personal change through the design and use of alternative assessment. These chapters were written by Hudson Valley Portfolio Assessment participants. Among them are a first-grade teacher, a sixth-grade teacher, a special education teacher and administrator, a director of language arts, and four high school English teachers. However, their roles—for the purposes of this book—are inconsequential. We have chosen these eight stories because they embody the changes that many Hudson Valley Project participants have experienced. The eight authors focus more on their own change processes and on their personal responses to learning about assessment than on the specific uses to which they put portfolios and performances. They embody different journeys into the process of reexamining professional practice.

The last part of this book includes an extensive chapter on the overall impact of the Hudson Valley Project on teachers' thinking and practice. It also underscores the limitations of the program in terms of producing systemic change in schools.

This book includes many practical ideas related to helping teachers design and use alternative assessment. It also showcases what many educators would call "best practice." Yet it should not be characterized as a "how to" or as a "success stories" book; its overriding purpose is to document a change process. As such, it is best suited for readers who want to implement alternative assessments and study their impact, or for those who want to participate in professional development experiences that focus on an examination and improvement of conditions that support teaching and learning.

1

The Unfolding of the Hudson Valley Portfolio Assessment Project

Giselle O. Martin-Kniep

The Hudson Valley Portfolio Assessment Project began in 1993 with a question and a conversation that emerged out of a formal presentation on school reform delivered to a cohort of administrators whose charge was to implement and support in-service educational programs for New York State. Frustrations were high; change is not easy, pleasant, or comfortable.

I was a university professor at the time and was also working as a consultant for several school districts. There is much freedom associated with being a consultant in terms of what one can and cannot say. I used my role to provoke discussions framed around current research on school reform. In the midst of our discussion, someone asked me a pivotal question: What was my vision for the kind of professional development that would result in changed assessment practices? I alluded to a series of assumptions I believed were paramount in designing and refining staff development.

Intrigued by the possibilities, a group of seven Boards of Cooperative Education Services (BOCES)[1] administrators invited me to a meeting to further explore our ideas. I was also intrigued and began to muse privately over the possibilities of what it might mean to implement these assumptions—to turn ideas into practice and beliefs into actuality. The meeting occurred a few weeks later, each of us inspired by the possibility of creating a distinctive staff development project and admittedly frightened by the ominous task being proposed. The Hudson Valley Portfolio Assessment Project (HVPAP) was born.

1. BOCES are regional curriculum and staff development agencies who serve as liaisons between the New York State Department of Education and the school districts in New York State.

Today, I am surrounded by the treasures produced by this venture and by the huge responsibility to do justice to moments that have convinced me of the power of dreams. Needless to say, the task is greater than my ability to capture all that needs to be said. The tremendous successes of the project were a result of a particular constellation of people and events.

The Players

Program participants were recruited through two regional presentations that I made in April 1993 to more than two hundred teachers and administrators affiliated with seven regional BOCES. These presentations were followed by an application and commitment process that included having each teacher respond to five different questions:

1. What excites you the most about teaching writing? Briefly describe one of your most successful writing instruction activities.

2. Describe how you currently assess student writing.

3. After reading the project description and job responsibilities associated with HVPAP, describe what special skills you bring to the project.

4. Describe your background in the teaching/training of adults. What has been your most rewarding experience working with adults?

5. Describe your most significant personal noninstructional writing experience.

Each applicant also had to provide evidence of administrative support in the form of signed endorsements to participate in the project from both the school principal and the district's superintendent. Teachers who were selected to participate would commit to participate in project activities for three years and to complete all project requirements. In turn, they would receive a yearly stipend of $1000.00 and six release days during each year. School districts paid their respective BOCES $1500.00 per year for each participating teacher. In exchange for this investment, districts would have access to all project materials and resources and would be able to eventually have their own participating faculty play a role in the professional development of teachers within their district.

First year HVPAP participants included 101 teachers from fifty districts in seven counties from the mid–Hudson Valley region of New York. Most of the teachers were recruited and selected at the district level. In some instances, principals nominated teachers or asked specific teachers to volunteer. In other cases, a member of the central administration did the recruitment.

The recruitment process and supporting documents emphasized that this was a program for K–12 teachers in all subject areas but that its primary focus would be communication and literacy. We also stressed that we would give preference to teachers who had at least a basic understanding of and a strong interest in alternative forms of assessment. Most of the teachers in the project were experienced teachers, but their experience with alternative forms of assessment,[2] and their knowledge of different approaches to literacy and writing was, at best, uneven. Their working conditions also varied, and, more specifically, the degree of freedom the teachers had to use alternative assessments and process-based approaches to writing was diverse. In addition, the schools did not provide all teachers with the same support for their project-related work. This support included release time, access to copy machines and secretarial support, and paid planning time.

Participants included a microcosm of school district life: thirty elementary school teachers, eighteen middle school teachers, thirty-two high school teachers, eight special education teachers, thirteen language arts teachers (reading/writing specialists), eleven administrators, and eight special education teachers. Among the middle and high school teachers, there were twenty-six English teachers, six social studies teachers, four mathematics teachers, two technology teachers, one foreign language teacher, one science teacher, one speech and language pathologist, and one vocational education teacher. Based upon our prior experience with staff development, and realizing the importance of teachers supporting one another through a change process, we had encouraged districts to send a team of two teachers from the same building. In about one-third of the cases, however, the teams that were sent to the project were from different buildings.

The program suffered some changes and attrition over time. Over a three-year period, we lost thirty teachers to budgetary constraints, illness, pregnancies, retirements, relocation, frustration, and burnout. Some of these teachers were replaced in the second year of the project, and we ended the third year with approximately eighty consistent participants.

Program staff included seven New York State BOCES administrators, whose role was to develop and implement staff development activities for their participating school districts. I functioned as the project designer and director, facilitating all program activities and supervising the work of additional presenters, consultants, and research staff. Even though I delivered 90 percent of the program content, in the second and third years of the project I invited two of my colleagues from Adelphi University, Diana M. Feige and Devin Thornburg, to support teachers with tutorials and clinics. I also invited another colleague and former teacher, Diane Cunningham, to assist me in the review of teacher portfolios and in the management of the data collected through different research activities.[3] Program consultants included Grant

---

2. Alternative assessment refers to any assessment that is not a paper-and-pencil and selected response test.

3. The research activities we engaged in included a three-year study of students' writing across grade levels, and an analysis of themes and patterns of change revealed in the teachers' journals and other reflective entries over the course of three years.

Wiggins, director of CLASS (Center for Learning, Assessment and School Structure); Suzi Grodin, a writing expert and Dean of the School of Education at the University of Massachusetts in Amherst; and David Jackson, former Superintendent of Shoreham Wading School District in Long Island, New York. Research staff included two doctoral candidates in psychology from Adelphi University, Judith Luwish and Peter Piepgrass, and Margot Diekmann, a doctoral candidate in the School of Education at Teachers College, Columbia University. In our first year we also invited several teachers from North Shore School District in Long Island, New York, with whom I had worked in a three-year action research and assessment design project, to share their assessments.

Assumptions Underlying the Program

What began as a response to a spontaneous question became the frame for the three-year project. As the warning goes, be careful of what you wish for—it may come true. The assumptions alluded to in early 1993—informed by years of research and program evaluation and development that focused on teacher and student change—had shaped a staff development project involving more than one hundred school teachers and administrators by June 1993. As dynamic and flexible as the project was, the following set of assumptions grounded us and permeated every program and activity.

Collaborative Communities of Teachers-as-Learners Can Help Teachers Initiate, Support, and Sustain Significant Changes in Their Practices

Teacher professional development is most effective when teachers are immersed in communities of learning. Creating such communities is difficult even in the best of circumstances, especially when we consider that schools seldom operate as learning communities for teachers. The very structure and rhythm of schools make opportunities for adult conversations about teaching and learning practically nonexistent. Whereas schools are constantly inundated with numerous innovations and materials, teachers who have taught for five or more years have realized that these are rarely accompanied by the needed focus and organizational support to become fully implemented. Moreover, the conservative nature of schools as institutions, with socialization being the primary goal, leaves little freedom for teachers to stray from institutionally sanctioned mores. In light of these factors, we must provide teachers with safe places for change.

The only alternative to district- and schoolwide systemic efforts toward change is the creation of communities of teachers who can experience a learning process together to develop a common vision for themselves as learners, and work toward a common goal. In these communities, teachers could share common questions and concerns about their work and grapple with critical issues such as grading fairly or devising ways to produce learning among increasingly heterogenous groups of students.

Creating learning communities is no easy feat. Such communities are a function of a group's composition and of the chemistry and dynamics of their participants. They require access to ongoing opportunities for informal and structured discussion, and they are highly dependent upon a shared vision and a belief in the possibility of collaboratively constructed learning.

Reflection Can Help Teachers and Students Learn and Grow

New learning provokes dissonance and discomfort. It makes us feel inadequate and uncertain. It leads us to question what we once considered to be true. Learning is about not knowing exactly where we are going or about how we are going to get there. Perhaps the greatest challenge we face as learners is the need to accept that we cannot learn fast enough or well enough to avoid mistakes along the way. For some reason, even though we believe that student learning is about thinking, producing, editing, revising, and producing again and again, we do not often permit ourselves to apply the process to our own learning. We want to translate what we learn into complete and tidy products and activities for our students, and more than anything else, we want to get it right. But our teaching and assessment practices and activities are never independent of our own learning about them, and just as it is necessary for students to tinker and experiment, it is imperative that teachers do so as well. In an atmosphere replete with the pretense of a clearly developed technology of teaching, learning, and assessment tools, it is extremely difficult for educators to value their own learning development. We need to grapple with our learning processes by reminding ourselves that the journey into the development of credible and valid assessments is ongoing. We need to reinforce the belief that real learning is about asking more and deeper questions and not about having clear and definite answers.

In this context, assessment design is a work in progress, with each of our assessments reflecting where we are and what we are comfortable with at a particular moment in our own development as learners. Our goal as developers and users of an appropriate assessment repertoire should be to design assessment tools that are congruent with our educational philosophy and practice. The question teachers should ask as learners of assessment is not, Is this assessment good? but rather, Does this assessment do greater justice than prior assessments to what I truly value?

Reflection is the primary means by which we can become learners, and systematic inquiry serves as the basis for communicating this learning to others. These activities, in turn, allow us to articulate the essence of our own professionalism. Only after we have had opportunities to investigate our work can the more practical aspects of assessment training be addressed and understood. Because learning is often an uncomfortable and difficult process, we need support in the form of access to peers who are going through similar learning experiences. We need time for and access to ongoing training, which can help us probe deep enough into our professional practice to improve it.

Reflection is a luxury that we rarely afford ourselves. We live in a society that places a much higher premium on the production of work and paper than on the quality of that work. Time is something to be managed and conquered, and this conquest means that more and more needs to be done. As a teacher, I often found myself yielding to the temptation to "cover" the material I planned to teach, even though I realized that such coverage could compromise my students' ability to learn. Such compromise was particularly evident when I deprived my students of opportunities to actively engage with and process new material. The pressure to teach more content in a school calendar that is already too fragmented, and to prepare students to do well on exams that span a wide array of surface knowledge, precludes teachers from creating the needed space for them and their students to ponder the value and meaning of their learning.

If we believe that assessment should extend and even produce learning, then teachers need to help students process and reflect upon their learning by experiencing and modeling the reflective process themselves. We model the reflective process when we share our work and analyze our students' feedback and when we document our learning over time with professional portfolios of our evolving experimentation with curriculum, instruction, and assessment.

Alternative Assessment Can Be Used as a Lever for the Alignment of Teachers' Curriculum, Instruction, and Assessment Practices

It is so difficult to articulate the specific purpose of our daily work in the classroom—or to explain just what it is that a certain book or lesson will contribute to a student's understanding or ability to do something with that learning. The daily work of teaching precludes many of us from seriously considering the relative merits of our curriculum. Discriminating the essential from the superficial is imperative in our expanding world of information, but schools do not provide or even openly endorse the time and space to do that.

If we are to create a diversified assessment system that can include the use of portfolios, processes, performance, and authentic assessments,[4] we need to do more than tinker with curriculum and instruction. We need to de-

---

4. *Authentic assessment* refers to tasks that require students to engage with real or plausible problems and challenges. These problems are contextualized and require that students use knowledge and skills to engage in disciplined inquiry and present their learning to an audience that could naturally use or care about the information presented. *Portfolios* are purposeful collections that exhibit the efforts, progress, and achievement of learners in one or more areas. *Process assessment* is the assessment of students' thinking about their learning or performance. *Outcomes* are statements that define what students ought to know, be able to do, or value. These statements are observable, measurable, or inferable, and are stated in results-focused terms.

velop a process to help us identify essential learning outcomes for our students and to align our curriculum and assessment to those outcomes. We also need an open forum for the discussion of texts and learning experiences. Such discussion might allow us to discriminate those aspects of our curriculum and instruction that deserve more time and space from those that should be minimized or abandoned. In essence, we need to give ourselves permission to question and reinvent what and how we teach and assess.

Assessment Can Only Be Understood or Developed in Conjunction with Supporting Curriculum and Instruction

Assessments are not just a set of tools that we can add to teachers' curriculum and instruction. They are intrinsically tied to what teachers value, what they teach, the amount of control over learning they share with students, and what they think they are responsible for measuring.

Good assessment cannot exist without good instruction. It would be no more inappropriate to use a multiple-choice test to assess students' ability to recognize the multiple perspectives involved in a debate than it would be to ask students to write a letter to an editor using twenty newly introduced vocabulary words. In both of these cases, there is a mismatch between the learning and the assessment demands. Indeed, the design and use of appropriate assessments involves a unique and fairly well-developed body of knowledge of design, rubric development, use of exemplars, validity, and reliability. However, this knowledge cannot be delivered outside a much broader context that includes teachers' beliefs about learning and assessment. If it is, we are likely to co-opt and subvert alternative assessments to teaching practices and curriculum that, in many schools, are already too focused on students' memorization and use of decontextualized knowledge and skills. A portfolio containing teacher-selected dittos does not provide a richer portrayal of a student's learning than the independent presentation of the dittos themselves.

Assessment and Teaching Practices Are and Should Be Deeply Individualized and Personal

The assessments teachers use are a reflection of their knowledge base about content, learning, and assessment; of their beliefs about the appropriate audiences and uses of assessment data; and of their real or perceived pressures to document a particular learning outcome.

Changing teachers' educational beliefs and philosophy is not easy; it occurs only when mirrors are provided for teachers to see themselves and their work from the perspective of the other: the student. When teachers learn about assessment and learning, they must be able to process the material by applying it to their own teaching, receive constructive feedback on their understanding and use of this knowledge and skills, and continuously improve upon their work in an atmosphere that encourages trust and risk taking—an atmosphere that celebrates the notion of teacher-as-learner.

To embrace what has come to be understood as constructivist and student-centered learning, we (teachers and students) need to be aware of our own learning. We must be comfortable with the fact that in a room full of people, nobody hears or understands the same thing. We must invest time in a learning process that includes reflection, introspection, and systematic inquiry.

Learning can only occur when we can actively incorporate material into our practice. All learners bring some knowledge and skill to a new experience. Teachers at professional development programs are no exception. Rather than assuming that they simply need to learn new knowledge and skills, we need to offer them continuous opportunities to articulate what they already know and do and to juxtapose their experience with new material about learning and assessment. These opportunities include reviewing teacher-developed and other student assessments, critiquing them from the standpoint of their usefulness and demands, and comparing them with the kinds of assessments and learning experiences they currently use.

When I first began my work as a staff developer, I often heard the claim that teachers disliked theoretically grounded presentations and favored instead professional development experiences from which they derived concrete, usable, and specific classroom-related activities. Having spent more than seven years in the world of teaching and teacher education, I have come to understand that this does not mean that teachers need ready-made curriculum materials or cookie-cutter assessment tools. In my own interplay with students and teachers, I have never been able to use any lesson in the same way twice or to duplicate the same experience as I move from one classroom to another. Working with students is like a dance. A different partner can make all the difference. And the dance is never the same. Moods change, pressures accumulate, and group dynamics make or break the best crafted activity.

Teachers' Concerns About and Use of Alternative Assessments Mirror Their Own Developmental Processes as Learners

A most significant shift in teachers' assessment-related knowledge, beliefs, and practices occurs when teachers transform their teacher-centered assessments into student-driven ones. When teachers are first exposed to alternative assessments such as portfolios and authentic measures, they often question their use in light of the time demands that such assessments impose. They are skeptical about the public's acceptance of those assessments, since they seem to be so much more subjective than traditional paper-and-pencil and machine-scored tests. They doubt students' ability to generate scoring criteria and develop rubrics, and they question students' capacity to reflect accurately upon and evaluate their own work. Even though many teachers I have worked with have found student-developed portfolios to be richer and more informative than teacher-developed portfolios, more often than not they have initiated their journey into portfolio assessment with the creation of teacher-directed portfolios.

Similarly, even though the products derived from the use of authentic assessments are multifaceted, original, and demanding, teachers struggle with finding a fit for those assessments in the context of a curriculum that is, for the most part, anything but authentic. These early attempts are by no means a waste of time, nor should they be minimized. They are akin to students' initial exploration with the written word. Just as students develop the capacity to write for different audiences and purposes with the assistance of coaching and practice, so do teachers develop an increased and more sophisticated assessment repertoire.

Alternative Assessments Can Help Us Reconcile Competing Educational Goals

It is baffling to realize that we function in a school system that has historically operated with conflicting goals: providing all students with access and opportunity to learn *and* identifying and sorting those who will succeed and those who will not. In general, the system is replicating a society that appears to be more democratic than it truly is. It is even more surprising that we can pretend to reconcile these goals in our own classrooms and continue to support a perception that schools are rational institutions with explicitly shared codes and regulations. We don't lack reminders of the inherent conflicts embedded in these irreconcilable goals. The moral dilemmas we face during marking periods and grading exercises bring these contradictions forth. Silence governs as we create idiosyncratic mechanisms to protect students who need protection, punish those who need to be reminded that we are in power, and reward the ones who have fulfilled expectations that we only made explicit to ourselves when we saw the power and quality of their completed work.

Traditional paper-and-pencil assessments favor a certain kind of learner and learning. They are best suited for assessing recall-based knowledge and for students who have acquired the skills and tricks associated with doing well on such tests, which demand the isolated recall of knowledge or the use of specific skills in a predefined time period.

Alternative assessment cannot solve the inherent conflicts of grading and evaluation in schools, but it can provide us with a more diversified set of tools and processes for managing these conflicts. These include learning opportunities that are suited to a variety of learning styles and dispositions, using assessment tools that provide students with different paths for demonstrating their knowledge and skills, and using rubrics and scoring criteria that guide students in the production and evaluation of their work. The net effect of these tools is a more purposeful teaching and evaluation system and scaffolding structure that enables different students to produce quality work.

Explicit Subjectivity and Data-Driven Judgments Should Replace the Pretense of Objectivity

We have come to believe that subjectivity is a problem in our practice because our testing programs assume objectivity and rationality. We have also lacked needed evidence to support what we believe students know or can do. In our practice as teachers, we face a grading and reporting system that reduces our students to letters and numbers and prevents them and us from showcasing students' unique learning styles, abilities, and dispositions.

All assessment is inherently subjective. Whereas some aspects of human learning entail greater subjectivity in judgment than others—for example, discerning whether or not a student's poster involves creative use of media versus determining whether students can measure the width of a desk—all learning and its assessment involve human judgment subject to bias. The decision to include specific content and skill items on a test, as well as the choice on what option responses to include, are inherently subjective, even though the test will be scored by a machine. Thus, rather than assume that we can create objective assessments, we must accept our subjectivity as a given, make it known to our students, and ground our judgments on products and performances that meet real-world standards.

When assessment is standardized and externally imposed, it robs teachers and students of its instrumental value, and, more specifically, of the opportunity to use assessment data as a means to extend and not just measure learning. Teachers need to use assessment as an ally. They need to develop an assessment repertoire that allows them to document what many of them intuitively know about students but for which they lack any tangible evidence. They need to use assessments that measure not what is easy to count but what is worth measuring. Finally, they need to gather and manipulate assessment information that enables their students to determine what they know and what they need to know next. In short, they need an assessment system than honors and substantiates the richness of learning as a process and a product. To do this, teachers need to be very clear about what they want students to learn and do. They then need to assume an active role in shaping their curriculum around their goals for student learning and in aligning it to their instruction and assessment practices.

Teachers Can and Should Play a Role in Teaching Other Teachers

Despite the importance of theoretically and research-based knowledge about teaching and learning, such a knowledge base lacks the context-grounded experiences only classroom teachers possess. Only teachers know what it feels like to use a scoring rubric[5] for the first time, or what it takes to get students to articulate the reasons for selecting a specific sample of their work by linking such reasons to the specific standards that informed its development. Only teachers can discuss the experience of having students collect and analyze their work over time, and only they can talk about the fears and anxiety associated with changing their assumptions about students, learning, and assessment.

Teachers need to identify and use their own learning about classroom assessment as a vehicle for helping other teachers do the same thing. If teachers engage each other in substantive conversations about the process of assessment development, they can begin to counteract current forces for assessment standardization and generate collective teacher-generated processes for documenting and assessing the development and quality of student work. Their own professional portfolios can be their primary tool for such collective processes and for the development of their role as professional developers.

---

5. A rubric is a scoring tool that defines and differentiates among levels of performance.

2

Program Components of the Hudson Valley Portfolio Assessment Project

Giselle O. Martin-Kniep

Assumptions cannot be grounded without supporting program elements. First, the BOCES administrators and I sought to develop teachers' knowledge and skills in the area of alternative assessment. Over time, teachers were to develop classroom assessments centered on a broad range of communication outcomes. Second, we wanted to discover and discuss what good communication looked like across subjects and grade levels. To do this, we sought to identify student work that embodied high standards and to use such work to help teachers and students work toward such standards. Finally, we wanted teachers to help other teachers learn about and develop their own classroom assessments. We hoped to achieve this by enabling teachers to study and document their own learning processes via professional portfolios that they would use, in turn, to teach others.

The program was inaugurated in June 1993 with a full-day session on portfolio and authentic assessment followed in July 1993 by the first of three summer institutes. In between these institutes, participants came together for six additional days of professional development work. These were spread out over the course of the year and occurred every six to eight weeks. In addition to these days, participants met for a few hours after school in regional clusters of about twenty-five teachers on a monthly basis to discuss issues related to assessment and to support each other's work.

The program components changed over time, mostly because the Hudson Valley Project planning group—the seven BOCES administrators and I—would gather after each program event to use our own insights as well as participants' feedback to plan future activities. Thus, whereas our goals remained the same throughout the history of the project, the path to these goals was adjusted continuously. For example, after our second summer institute, and as we began to undergo some attrition and replacement of project participants, we began to individualize our program. In addition to providing the group with input sessions, followed by small- and large-group work time, we instituted the use of clinics and tutorials. Clinics consisted of one- or two-hour sessions designed to provide newcomers to the project or teachers whose assessment design shared similar problems with opportunities to acquire further knowledge and skills and to use this learning to solve the specific assessment difficulties they had. Tutorials involved conferences between project staff and individual teachers using the teacher's teacher-as-learner portfolio.

Program Components and Their Evolution

Input Sessions

Much of our first program year was characterized by input sessions in which we explored a number of assessment-related topics, including assessment purposes and measures, portfolio assessment, outcome development, rubric design, teacher inquiry and action research, and writing assessment. I began a typical input session with a presentation of key ideas related to a topic, followed by specific classroom-related illustrations and an opportunity for participants to discuss and apply the material learned. For example, when I introduced the topic of outcome-based assessment design, I included a rationale for outcomes as the basis for design. I then described the attributes of outcomes and indicators and presented a series of examples that linked outcomes, indicators, learning and assessment opportunities, and performance criteria. After a brief discussion among participants, we engaged in a two-hour activity that included the following steps. First, we identified some of the attributes that define our local communities, our state, our nation, and the world as a whole. We then described the knowledge, skills, and dispositions that graduates from our schools will need to function effectively in the world in which they will live. These statements embodied learner outcomes, that is, statements that define what students ought to know, be able to do, or value in results-focused terms. In small groups comprised of teachers working in similar grade levels, we identified the specific manifestations of such learner outcomes for specific groups of students. Finally, we asked individual teachers to identify the kinds of learning experiences and assessment tasks that might demonstrate students' attainment of desired outcomes.

Over the life of the project, we revisited many topics once or even twice. This was especially true for the topics of portfolio and authentic assessment; as teachers developed and used different assessments, new questions would arise.

Showcase and Analysis of Exemplary Work

Whereas alternative assessment was a much-discussed topic among educational researchers and policy makers in 1993, there were few good examples of classroom-based authentic performance and portfolios. Most of the resources in these areas included assessments being developed for Vermont, Kentucky, Maryland, and California, or by efforts such as the Coalition of Essential Schools or Harvard's Project Zero and Arts Propel. In our first project year, we provided teachers with many of these resources but used them primarily as springboards for our own designs rather than as models to emulate.

We then began to generate outcomes and indicators and used them to link teachers to current teaching and assessment practices. This design process was documented via a teacher-as-learner portfolio. We asked teachers to include the following sets of materials in their portfolio.

1. Outcomes addressed by student portfolios or performances you are designing. What is/are the assessment(s) trying to document? What indicators support the attainment of these outcomes? Where does the assessment fit into the overall curriculum?

2. Description of student portfolio or assessment tasks: time line; content focus; participants; kinds of entries [allowed or required]; time devoted to each entry; role of student, parent; etc. Rubrics and grading devices used to assess the portfolio or performance components, or the portfolio/performance as a whole. (Includes a copy of all the assessment drafts generated in the course of the year.)

3. Profile of your classroom and school, including salient demographic factors (socio-economic status, cultural diversity, kind of school, etc.).

4. Profile of three to five target students. In what ways do these students capture the diversity of your classroom?

5. Description of lessons/activities that precede/lead/follow portfolio or performance entries.

6. Student portfolios/performances or students profiled and additional student work if necessary (especially exemplary work).

7. Dated journal of activities related to the design and implementation of action research project using portfolios. Includes comments on:

    a. Students' reaction to/performance with tasks or portfolio entries

    b. Time required to administer/score/comment on portfolio/task (separate log if necessary)

    c. Reactions or questions related to your use of alternative assessments

8. Optional entry.

Between the completion of our first year and our second summer institute, we identified fifteen teacher portfolios that we deemed exemplary in terms of their explicitness, thoroughness, and quality. At our second summer institute we showcased these exemplars and provided teachers with several opportunities to analyze and discuss them. At the same time, we brought in outside teachers who were also in the process of implementing alternative assessments in their classrooms, and we organized various roundtable discussions so that teachers who taught at different grade levels and subjects would be exposed to assessment designs that were relevant in their own teaching contexts.

The showcasing and analysis of teacher portfolios continued throughout the life of the project. At our third summer institute we displayed more than thirty portfolios, and in our last project event, in June 1996, we were able to draw from about sixty different designs, even though some of these were developed by teachers who did not join the project until the second year.

In addition to collecting, analyzing, and displaying exemplary teacher designs, we showcased student work to reveal exemplary communication attributes in different grade levels and school contexts. We had two mechanisms for identifying and using student exemplars from teachers' classrooms. In each of the project years, we asked all participants to administer this writing prompt to one of their classes:

> Sometimes we try to do the right thing and it does not work out. Write about
> a time when this happened to you. If this were to happen again, what would
> you do differently?

We used the student work collected to examine the impact of the project on students' writing and reflection and to identify and discuss exemplary student writing in different grade levels. We produced two collections of this work and used them in our second and third project years as resources for teachers to use in their own classrooms and in their professional development activities.[1]

As our project unfolded and teachers became increasingly proficient in the implementation of rich and authentic learning experiences, we began to collect and use student work during our project sessions. At our second and third summer institutes, teachers submitted material from students they considered exemplary. We developed a systematic process for the review and evaluation of this work. This process consisted of having teachers work in grade-level clusters (primary, upper elementary, middle school, and high school by subject) to examine and annotate each of the student samples. In their annotation, they determined whether the work was exemplary by using a three-point rating scheme: 1 (definitely not an exemplar), 2 (undecided), and 3 (a definite exemplar). They also described the reasons for their judgment. If they believed the work was exemplary, they identified what it was an exemplar

---

1. For information and cost of these collections, write to the Putnam/Northern Westchester BOCES, 200 BOCES Dr., Yorktown Heights, NY 10598.

of. If they did not believe the work was exemplary, they stated the ways in which it fell short of desired standards. They also identified the kinds of specific information that would have helped determine with certainty if the work was exemplary.

Following the showcasing of student work, we discussed the ways in which teachers conveyed standards for performances and products with their students, and the role that exemplars could play in guiding students' thinking and performance. We also discussed the various ways in which exemplars would impact curriculum and instruction.

Assessment Feedback and Refinement Processes

In the initial absence of exemplary teacher-as-learner portfolios classroom assessments, we developed several mechanisms for reviewing, critiquing, and refining the work teachers generated. These included:

1. Letter exchanges and reviews and critiques of assessment drafts
2. Tutorials and clinics during our program sessions in the second and third years
3. Self- and peer reviews of teacher-as-learner portfolios

When the project began, much of the feedback on the assessments took the form of letter exchanges between participants and myself. In these letters, I would comment on the merits of the work produced and raise questions about the meaning and value of the assessments. I would end each letter with suggestions on possible improvements, bearing in mind where each teacher was in his or her readiness to move from teacher-driven to learner-centered assessment approaches.

As the project unfolded and we all began to discover the specific attributes of quality that comprised the teacher-as-learner portfolios and assessment designs, we developed a scoring and review process that I, the teachers, and additional outside reviewers used throughout the project. This process consisted of two different versions of a protocol for the review of teacher-as-assessor portfolios (see Appendix A) and two different versions of a protocol for the review of accompanying student portfolios (see Appendix B). We developed these two different versions to accommodate teachers' preferences for the kinds of feedback they wanted to give and receive about their teacher and student portfolios. Some teachers preferred open-ended questions and answers whereas others liked using a checklist format.

Notwithstanding the value of teachers' receiving feedback about their work from either myself or other project consultants, it was the teachers' own peer review of each other's work that became one of the most powerful mechanisms for teachers to learn about portfolio design and to help each other achieve common goals. At the end of each project year we held one or two peer review sessions, which were followed by opportunities for teachers to incorporate other teachers' feedback into their assessment designs. To prepare teachers for these reviews we developed a training video of the review process.

Toward the end of our last project year, we were also able to develop four different holistic rubrics to describe and differentiate among the qualities of the different sections of a teacher's portfolio. These rubrics correspond to different areas of teacher expertise: teacher-as-learner, teacher-as-researcher, teacher-as-curriculum-and-assessment-designer, and teacher-as-professional-developer. These rubrics are included in Appendix C.

Reflection Activities

In addition to enabling teachers to reflect upon their work via the review of their assessment designs and teacher portfolios, we provided them with ongoing opportunities to document their thinking and learning. When the project began, we gave each teacher a journal. We encouraged them to write about their thinking and learning at each program session and whenever they took time to work on their assessments. We also asked them to complete journal questions prior to several of our programs. Finally, we asked them to complete reflective logs during each of the summer institute days. The following assignment is one example.

> Prepare a journal entry. This entry should include your reflections on something that you have learned since you began your involvement in this project. We are particularly interested in learning if any of your assumptions and/or knowledge about students, learning, assessment, curriculum, etc. have changed as a result of your participation.

The reflective logs assignments often looked something like this:

Log 1

1. In what ways, if any, have you changed the way in which you teach writing this year as a result of your participation in the Hudson Valley Portfolio Assessment Project?
2. What, if anything, has surprised you about your students' writing this year?
3. Have there been any changes in how your students tend to feel about writing?

Log 2

1. In what ways, if any, have there been changes in the outcomes you expect from your students in the area of communication as a result of your participation in the Hudson Valley Portfolio Assessment Project?
2. What changes, if any, have you made in the communication-related assignments you give your students?

3. What changes, if any, have you made in the kinds of responses you give to your students' writing? Please indicate the type and source (e.g., yourself, peers, other teachers, teacher aides, etc.).

Log 3

1. What have you learned about assessment in the course of participating in the Hudson Valley Portfolio Assessment Project?

2. What questions do you now have regarding each of the following areas:

    a. The tests and assessments you use

    b. Your students' learning

    c. Your grading practices

    d. The relationship between the tests and assessments you use and your grading practices

Here is an example of an activity.

Shoebox Activity

1. Identify one artifact that captures the essence of your learning in the project and be prepared to discuss its meaning.

2. Complete the following writing assignment and include it in the shoebox with the artifact.

    a. What are the successes associated with using alternative assessment (portfolios, performances, and processes) you have experienced? Use imagery and/or any form of narration (story, fable, or fairy tale) to describe these successes for you and your students.

    b. Describe some of the aspects of using alternative forms of student assessment that are not so successful or satisfying. Even though you may identify several aspects, concentrate on one or two. To describe it, use an interior monologue; a dialogue; or a letter to students, peers, or parents.

Teacher-Driven Professional Development Activities

We used a number of strategies to enable teachers to use their own processes to facilitate the work of other teachers. One such strategy involved inviting administrative staff from all participating districts along with project participants to regional programs held each of the project years. These programs included an update of our progress, presentations by as many as three teachers about their assessments and learning processes, and working sessions centered on a discussion of ways to use project participants in in-school and district staff development activities. These meetings were critical because district staff were eager to "use" participants as resources, yet they did not know how to do so appropriately. For example, early in the project, several school administrators wanted teachers to make presentations to the school district's board of education or to teach a workshop to teachers during district conference dates. At the time this expectation was premature since much of our first eighteen months of work was centered on opening the world of assessment to teachers while at the same time enabling them to question their own practices. During this period, participants were often frustrated and anxious, feeling they were in no position to tell other teachers what to do.

In one of our most successful programs we invited an elementary school teacher, a middle school team, and a high school teacher to be part of a panel presentation. Each of these participants brought along three students. Using a combined town meeting and panel format, teachers, students, and members of the audience engaged in a wonderful discussion about the value of portfolio assessment. Most impressive was a conversation among students from different grade levels who discovered, perhaps for the first time, the common threads that link all learners.

Several times in the project we also engaged participants in simulations so they would better appreciate some of the subtleties and intricacies related to assessment design and assessment policy. These simulations presented participants with opportunities to discover multiple perspectives related to topics such as the use of different kinds of assessment in the classroom, the different and often conflictive purposes that assessment can serve, and the kinds of assumptions made by different kinds of teachers and administrative staff about the work involved in assessment design. One of our simulations is described in Appendix D.

To further prepare teachers for their role as professional developers we invited a group of participants to a two-day working retreat. There we gathered, selected, and adapted assessment-related resource material. This material was compiled into a series of staff development modules that was distributed to all program participants early on in our third project year. These modules included resource materials and professional development activities in the areas of:

1.   Authentic assessment
2.   Value and uses of different kinds of portfolios
3.   Value of student self-assessment and reflection
4.   Representative rubrics

In addition, we administered a survey of professional development activities that allowed us to monitor the kinds of activities that project participants were involved in and the issues that they were facing. These are the questions we asked:

1.   Since you became involved with the HVPAP have you been asked to share anything related to your work on the project?

Yes

No

2. Since you became involved with the HVPAP have you volunteered to share anything related to your work on the project?

Yes
No

Please complete the following questions for up to three of the most significant events in which you shared project-related information or materials.

3. If you were asked to present, who asked you?

4. Who was the audience?

5. What was the duration (e.g., one twenty-minute presentation at a faculty meeting, ongoing two-hour meetings after school once a month, etc.)?

6. How many people were actively involved in the audience?

7. When did this take place?

8. What resources/materials (if any) did you share? Please enclose a set of these.

9. To what extent do you think that your presentation/sharing was effective?

not at all 1 2 3 4 5 very effective

10. What feedback did you receive from the audience?

11. Were there any requests for follow-up?

Yes
No

12. In retrospect, what, if anything, would you have done differently if you had the opportunity to do so?

13. What specific resources or information would help you become more effective as a presenter?

14. Additional comments:

Finally, to facilitate teachers' ability to communicate with one another outside the project and to enable district administrative staff to contact teachers from different schools, we developed an annotated profile handbook of all project participants. This handbook included their grade level, school and district, the subject(s) they taught, their research question, and the focus of their alternative assessment. If a teacher's portfolio design was considered particularly thorough in terms of addressing the components of our review protocols, we noted that in the handbook.

The Learning Continues

The preceding program components speak to a demanding and comprehensive approach to staff development. Looking back, I am awestruck by what was accomplished, both in quantity and quality. The professional and philosophical risks taken by the coordinators and teachers were many; the dedication, courage, and caring support nurtured over the three years were outstanding. As the project concluded on June 4, 1996, we realized that many teachers wanted additional support and continued access to learning communities. Some of this support will be informal, although we intend to develop additional structured programmatic activities. The first of these programs, the Hudson Valley Leadership and Assessment Academy, which began in the summer of 1996, was implemented in the 1996–1997 school year. Two other programs, the Center for the Study of Expertise in Teaching and Learning, in Nassau BOCES Long Island, and the CLASSIC Capacity Building Initiative, in Hilton, New York, are currently underway. Both of these initiatives are designed to help teachers assume leadership roles in the areas of curriculum and assessment development within their districts.

The Hudson Valley Project has enabled me, the BOCES administrators, and more important, the teachers to assert the power of teachers-teaching-teachers. At the same time, the project established that participants' credibility lies not in their knowing everything there is to know about assessment, but in their having experienced a long-term study of their changing practices over time.

Professional communities of learners do not happen by accident. Sometimes they don't happen by design, either. As with some of the classes we encounter, the dynamics among the players make the difference between a learning community and a classroom that never transcends the tensions inherent in its walls. An honest respect for the learner and for the dissonance and discomfort that accompany learning are as essential as the guiding premises that framed this chapter. Having time to experiment, question, and share are also key ingredients. In the Hudson Valley Project we were privileged. We had three years to learn about, develop, and refine assessments using a common design process that facilitated our conversations. Chapter 3 describes this process and its elements.

3

The Design Process

Giselle O. Martin-Kniep

If assessment cannot be developed outside of one's thinking and teaching, there has to be a way for these seemingly separate pieces of professional practice to come together. In my early attempts to work in schools on curriculum- and assessment-related efforts, I realized that connecting *why* we teach with what and how we teach and assess was a necessary prerequisite to working with any of these aspects separately. This chapter outlines the design process we used to guide teachers through the development of new forms of assessment. The process includes five key elements: learner outcomes, outcome indicators, learning opportunities, assessment tasks, and performance criteria and scoring rubrics (see Figure 3–1). This design process begins with an articulation of learner outcomes and indicators that guide the teacher's thinking in terms of defining appropriate curriculum and assessments. These outcomes are the basis for identifying specific learning opportunities and assessment tasks and processes that can elicit students' achievement and performance. The design of tasks leads to the identification of performance criteria and, in some cases, the use of scoring rubrics and exemplars—scales that define and differentiate levels of student performance on a task or process. Rubrics can help students understand the teacher's expectations and monitor their own performance.

Even though Figure 3–1 presents this process as linear, in practice the process is recursive, with teachers often moving back and forth from one component to another. It is not uncommon, for example, to use indicators as the basis for the development of standards and rubrics and then to redefine the learning opportunities to ensure that the students have enough background information and skills to succeed in the assessment. It is also fairly typical for teachers to design authentic assessments by analyzing the content and performance demands of powerful units of study and then to develop one or more supporting assessment tasks with accompanying criteria.

Figure 3–1
The Design Process

Learner Outcomes: What do I want students to know and be able to do?

↕

Outcome Indicators: What specific actions or performances would my students engage in if they were to attain desired learner outcomes?

↕

Learning Opportunities: What do I need to teach or have students experience so they will attain the outcomes?

↕

Assessment Tasks: What do I need to collect or administer to prove that students have grown toward and/or achieved desired outcomes?

↕

Performance Criteria and Scoring Rubrics: How will I communicate what mastery or accomplishment means? What is good enough in terms of student performance?

Learner Outcomes

Learner outcomes are statements that describe what students are able to do, know, or value as a result of their schooling. They are equivalent to many state and national standards in their scope and focus. These statements provide teachers with a framework from which to make informed decisions about how to best use available curriculum resources. They also shift teachers' attention from what needs to be taught to what students should learn, and they reorient teachers and schools to a curriculum that is present- and future-informed rather than one that replicates past practices. Learner outcomes remind us all that schooling should be intrinsically linked to the demands of a rapidly and ever-changing world, and that it is our responsibility to prepare students to meet such demands.

Outcomes are derived from educational goals, which are representations of shared cultural and societal values related to the purpose of education and schools. Sample goal statements include: Students will be critical thinkers; Students will be effective communicators; and Students will be responsible citizens in a democratic society. Goal statements respond to the question, What will students be educated as, or for? Teachers can generate outcomes for a specific grade level (e.g., Seventh-grade students will write a business letter); for a program (e.g., Students in this class will explore and effectively use the narrative and expository genres); or for the end of schooling (e.g., Upon completion of twelfth grade, students will effectively write, listen, and speak for social interaction).

To generate outcome statements, teachers often find it useful to imagine their best students and then describe their learning at the end of the year or upon graduation. Good outcome statements share the following attributes:

Reflect broad goals

Describe what students ought to know and be able to do

Use result-focused, observable, measurable, or inferable terms

Are developmental

Are comprehensive and broad enough to be interdisciplinary

Are flexible in terms of how students attain them

Are specific enough to form the basis for outcome indicators and performance standards

Some examples of learner outcomes include:

Students will communicate orally and in writing for different purposes and audiences using a variety of genres.

Students will read and listen attentively for information and understanding by anticipating, summarizing, interpreting, analyzing, and evaluating contextual information, including various literary types, other written material, and media.

Students will explain how their writing changes in order to take into account the differences among audiences.

Students will use writing as a strategy for personal learning and clarification of thinking.

Students will use mathematical concepts and skills to solve real-life problems.

Outcome Indicators

Because outcomes are often broad and apply to many subject areas, they are not immediately useful in terms of helping teachers decide what or how to teach and assess. Therefore, individual teachers need to operationalize outcomes into more specific outcome indicators. Indicators are statements that describe the specific knowledge, characteristics, and performances that are likely to demonstrate students' attainment of learner outcomes for a specific grade level and, in some cases, subject. In some settings, these statements are also known as *content standards*. The following example shows an outcome and some of its respective indicators developed for a twelfth-grade English class.

Outcome: Students will communicate for a variety of purposes and audiences and in a variety of genres.

Indicators: Varies writing to suit a variety of expository, narrative, and persuasive purposes.

Discusses in writing a given piece of literature with specific reference to plot, character, setting, theme, mood, and/or author's purpose.

Articulates the relationship between purpose and product for different kinds of writing.

Analyzes various pieces of work in terms of their development process, quality, end result, and/or changes that may be made.

Here is a different example of outcomes and indicators provided by a high school social studies teacher.

Outcome: Students will understand the role of citizenship in a democracy.

Indicators: Describes various roles that citizens play in a democratic system.

Analyzes social trends toward and factors associated with nonparticipation in the democratic process.

Analyzes the impact of social issues on students' roles as citizens.

The preceding indicators allow teachers to translate broad and fairly generic outcomes into specific content- and skill-related ideas that can more readily be translated into lessons and assignments. They also begin to suggest the kinds of performance criteria that may be used to judge the merits of student work.

After teachers have identified outcomes and indicators they can proceed to define the kinds of learning opportunities that will enable students to attain desired outcomes.

Learning Opportunities

Learning opportunities are the processes and activities that teachers will use to enable students to attain desired learning outcomes. Essentially, the teacher asks, What kinds of experiences must I provide so that my students can attain the outcomes I want from them? Teachers should state learning opportunities in sufficiently general terms, allowing for the emergence of "teachable moments" and avoiding redundancy. At the same time, learning opportunities should be specific enough so that teachers can use them to lay out the scope and sequence of their curriculum.

I prefer the term "learning opportunities" to *curriculum* because most of the curriculum materials used in schools are fairly generic and are not necessarily developed to suit the contexts and needs of specific classrooms. Teachers should engage in a serious and critical review of existing curriculum resources to select the specific lessons, activities, and assignments that are intrinsically related to and supportive of their learning outcomes.

Following are examples provided by Tom Kersting, a Hudson Valley Project participant, of learning opportunities associated with the outcome, Students will communicate for a variety of purposes and audiences and in a variety of genres.

> *College admission essay:* Students were shown some typical college admission essay prompts and responses, which we analyzed in class. I urged them to write a response to a specific prompt from one of the colleges to which they were applying. After two classes reviewing useful strategies for linking purposes and audiences (from the guidance counselors and me) and one day in the computer lab, they conferred in assigned peer groups on their drafts and met with me for conferences as needed. The next day they submitted their revised essays, which I critiqued and returned ungraded. They then wrote a process journal response to my critique and prepared to send their essays with their college application.

> *Senior memoir:* After I modeled the use of personal artifacts via my own "memory bag" to trigger memories, students were to prewrite in preparation for their personal narrative. They were to recount how some experience(s) from their pasts contributed to change, growth, or insight in their lives. It was to be a blend of narrative and exposition (interpretation). After several days in the computer lab, they shared their work in progress in conferring groups, consulting our criteria for evaluation (previously developed from an analysis of published memoirs). They wrote a process journal account of their work in progress. After several more days of revision in and out of class, they made "final" changes, submitted their memoir and wrote a memoir on the completed process. I critiqued the papers and returned them with categories checked on the rubric scale, but ungraded.

Tom's learning opportunities are comprehensive and purposeful. It is easy to see how both of these opportunities translate into potential evaluative activities. In fact, because Tom uses a portfolio to assess students' growth and achievement as readers, thinkers, and writers, students actually select materials derived from such learning opportunities to include. The materials are evaluated as part of the students' portfolios and then are transformed into formal evaluation data.

Depending on the extent to which teachers use authentic learning opportunities, they will have to invest more or less time designing authentic assessment tasks. If teachers rely primarily on teacher-centered pedagogical approaches or on fragmented curricular approaches that emphasize rote learning of isolated skills, they will have to work harder at designing alternative curriculum and assessment tasks and at transforming the nature of teacher-student interactions. Because of the time required to develop these tasks, teachers need to set short- and long-term design goals. We recommend that teachers design a limited number of tasks per year and allow two or three years for their continued refinement. Teachers should not assume that they can generate comprehensive portfolios or tasks for every segment of their curriculum in a short period of time.

Even more important than specifying learning and assessment opportunities is identifying the links between these opportunities and specific outcomes. For instance, teachers can identify each of their outcomes and supporting indicators on a matrix, followed by the learning and assessment opportunities that are associated with one or more outcomes. They can also develop curriculum maps, which list learning outcomes and indicators, concepts developed, sources used, assignments, and assessment tasks. The process of mapping and refinement should be parsimonious; only a few assessment tasks should be required to assess a large number of outcomes.

Assessment Tasks

Teachers can use learning opportunities to obtain assessment data. A teacher, for example, could use the videotape of a debate to assess students' ability to communicate their understanding of an issue. Alternatively, teachers can develop specific tasks or measures that are incorporated into students' learning experiences to determine if students have grown toward or attained desired learner outcomes. In any event, the merits of our assessments lie in their congruence and support of specific learning outcomes and indicators.

There are many learning outcomes and indicators for students. If we need to determine if students possess specific kinds of information and not whether they can use it, a paper-and-pencil or recall activity is more than sufficient. If we want to know if students can use specific skills or operations, we need to use performance assessment. If we want to see how students are processing information or making decisions, process journals or think-aloud activities are most appropriate. Authentic assessment demands the integration of all of these learning targets through comprehensive tasks. This form of assessment is most suitable in situations in which we want students to apply knowledge and skills learned to confront real or plausible challenges for specifically defined audiences and purposes.

Some of the questions that teachers should ask themselves as they consider the use of different assessments include:

Does the assessment require that students become engaged in high-quality work?

Does the assessment result in students' understanding and effective use of a concept, issue, skill, or problem?

Will the assessment provide students with meaningful learning opportunities?

Does the proposed assessment support the learning process for students and teachers?

Is the assessment generally formative (provides feedback during the learning process) or summative (provides a single judgment at the end)?

Is the assessment responsive to what we know about how children learn?

Will the assessment help students become the kinds of adults we want them to be?

The development of authentic tasks cannot be separated from specific learning experiences that are, in and of themselves, authentic. These attributes comprise authenticity in curriculum and assessment:

Engagement with complete and contextualized outcome-linked tasks. Authentic assessment tasks are derived from integrated and often interdisciplinary units that present students with real-life challenges for real purposes and audiences, rather than from decontextualized and isolated activities.

Disciplined inquiry and elaborate communication. Students are expected to search for in-depth and grounded understanding as opposed to surface knowledge. To accomplish such depth, they need to grapple with discipline-focused and interdisciplinary-based knowledge. This requires that teachers know enough about the disciplines and subjects to help students understand their core concepts and organizing structures. Because we learn best by communicating our learning, students need opportunities to present what they know through elaborate written, oral, or artistic communication.

Developmentally appropriate, flexible, and meaningful tasks. Learning is an individually and socially mediated-constructed activity, which students experience differently. Students learn best when given opportunities to build on their prior knowledge through developmentally appropriate tasks that they perceive as intrinsically interesting. Because students will prefer different kinds of assessment modalities, assessments should be constructed in ways that allow students to make their learning evident by using their preferred learning modality.

Student-driven learning through explicit and shared standards. Teachers assume the roles of mediators, coaches, and facilitators of learning rather than the roles of directors and managers. Student-driven learning cannot occur unless students know where they are going and what they are to accomplish. This means that students must know, prior to their grappling with real and plausible tasks, the specific standards and criteria that they are to meet to achieve success and produce quality work. This is accomplished through the analysis of models, identification of performance criteria, and development of scoring criteria or rubrics that can guide them in the production and evaluation of their own work.

Attention to individually and socially mediated learning and thinking processes. Students need to process, reflect upon, and evaluate their learning on an ongoing basis. Given that much of our learning is socially grounded, teachers need to discriminate between assessment experiences that are best suited for individual student assessment and those that are best suited for group assessment.

Finding the appropriate balance between the use of assessments and tests to meet a variety of purposes is by no means an easy task. Such balance requires clarity of purpose, deep understanding of one's own curriculum, and assessment literacy.

Examples of Assessment Tasks

Examples of authentic assessment tasks are varied across grade levels and subjects. In Jennifer Hammond-King and Kerry Dunn's multiage class of first and second graders, students prepare and perform a play based on a unit of the human body. They work individually and in groups developing scenes for the play, assisted by three parents. One is a professional scriptwriter who helps them prepare and integrate their script. A second parent is a musician who helps them write the songs and musical score. The third parent is an artist who helps students design the stages and props for the play. The play is rehearsed in front of a second-grade class that rates the performance in terms of clarity and delivery. It is then formally presented to a group of third and fourth graders who are preparing for a health unit.

In Betsy Flor and Joan Schlosser's fourth-grade class, students write a letter requesting admittance into their public school. They need to indicate why they think that they have the needed interests and skills. They also discuss one or more aspects of their learning with which they struggled in third grade and state goals that they consider will make them more successful as students.

In Barbara Vertucci's fifth-grade class, students write and send a persuasive letter to the principal making a request they feel would contribute to the well-being of the school community. The criteria for success include that:

1. The request is reasonable and attainable.
2. The principal understands the nature of the request and the reasons supporting it.
3. The principal agrees with the writer's rationale and considers (and if possible takes action in favor of) the request.

As a result of a three-day trip to Massachusetts, a group of seventh graders taught by Carol LaMonda writes an article for the school's newspaper. The article is based on an interview of one or two Plymouth Plantation residents. The interview addresses questions such as:

1. Reasons for having left England
2. Changes in job-related activities since leaving
3. Family background and history
4. Current religious, social, and economic activities

An editorial board comprised of the seventh-grade class and school newspaper staff selects and submits the best articles to the Plimouth Plantation tourism bureau.

In Larry Diulio's ninth-grade Global Studies class, students role-play by assuming the roles of marketing consultants competing for employment with a United States corporation that is seeking to expand its business in China. The company has no prior knowledge of Chinese culture. The assessment task involves having the marketing teams make formal presentation bids to the corporation at a China-U.S. Business Exposition. Students are urged to provide practical economic advice grounded in a thorough understanding of Chinese history, philosophy, literature, and culture. This advice should include specific trading scenarios that the business is likely to encounter.

Performance Standards, Scoring Criteria, and Exemplars

Explicit performance standards and scoring criteria provide teachers and students with powerful images of high-quality work. This is important because all too often we assign work without really knowing what students will produce. We may do this because we consider the assignment important, because students seem to like doing it, or because we have assigned the work in the past. In these cases, we tend to discover the attributes of quality work only after we encounter and grade the most exemplary work. The timing of this discovery does not allow us to help other students produce work of comparable quality.

Yet many students need to be guided toward producing work of good quality because the assignments are too far-removed from what students are familiar with in the outside world; because the assignments seem too vague or unclear; or because the students have not received specific information about the criteria guiding the assignment. When teachers accompany their assignments with clear and descriptive performance criteria and, when necessary, accompany such criteria with rubrics and models, they communicate their expectations for students' achievement in ways that students can understand and use. This, in turn, makes it possible for students to use the attributes of exemplary work to monitor their own performance and achievement and serves as a scaffolding for the continued refinement and improvement of their performance.

The process of designing performance standards is recursive. Teachers begin this process by examining existing models of high-quality work from the contexts in which the work is produced, such as published oral histories, fiction, or poetry. Such analysis leads to the identification of attributes that make such models exemplary. For example, after analyzing and defining the attributes of an excellent oral presentation, one teacher generated the following criteria:

> The material presented was well researched, accurate, and relevant; the presentation was well organized and supported by visuals or media that clarified or accentuated the most important points; the presentation was thought provoking and interactive, drawing where appropriate on the audience's questions or comments; the presenter was assertive, clear and understandable; the student provided both a context or introduction and a closure or conclusion to the presentation.

Rubrics

Once teachers know what they want in terms of quality, they can help students recognize quality indicators by having them review available models or exemplars. Then teachers can help students develop scoring schemes and rubrics that will assist them in the production and evaluation of their own work. Rubrics can be holistic, providing a single score for a complete product or performance, or analytic, scoring every aspect of a product or performance separately. Rubrics are most effective when they are developed with students and when they are based on a careful study of exemplars or models.

Scoring rubrics are advantageous for teachers and students because they:

1. Translate teachers' expectations for students' work and achievement in ways that students can independently utilize

2. Help teachers focus their instruction by clarifying what they want from students

3. Make it possible for students to identify the attributes of exemplary work and to discriminate among work that embodies different levels of quality

4. Help students monitor their own performance and achievement on an ongoing basis

5. Serve as scaffolding devices by assisting students in moving from one performance level to another

6. Allow other stakeholders—parents, resource staff, supervisors—to understand teachers' criteria for judging students' work

7. Assist in the justification and validation of grades

Because of the participatory nature of the rubric development process and given the scaffolding embedded in students' having images of work produced with different degrees of quality, rubrics often lead to greater success for students who normally would not perform as well. In addition, the sharing of rubrics with students, their families, and other teachers makes the evaluation system public and subject to healthy discussions about the kind and quality of learning we want for students. Tom Kersting portrays these effects in the following excerpt from his professional portfolio:

> I am pleased with the rubrics we have devised for each part of the [students'] portfolio. As intended, the evaluation (by both them and me) of their portfolio is less subjective, less "intuitive" than last year. In addition, because they are rooting their evaluation in the criteria of the rubric, they seem to be working to a higher standard than in the past, when the evaluations were "looser" and more subjective because they were not addressing scaled criteria. Finally, the mandated use of the rubrics, coupled with the range of standards across a 6-point scale, seem to foster increased reflections on their part, as if they now have more to say and an increased vocabulary with which to say it.

Rubrics can be created to assess processes (e.g., cooperative learning, discussions, critical thinking exercises, habits of mind); products (e.g., portfolios, research papers, museum exhibits, investigations, stories, poems, and other artistic products); and performances (e.g., oral presentations, storytelling performances, debates, and panels). Unfortunately, in the initial absence of multiple samples of students' work, it is difficult to generate precise scoring rubrics or even to determine precisely how many levels of performance should be described. Thus, teachers should assume that initial rubrics are subject to significant revision. After using a rubric for the first time, they can refine it by stacking students' work into piles that share similar characteristics. By analyzing and describing how the stacks are different from one another, teachers can enhance the description of the rubric levels, help students use the rubrics to monitor their work, and provide more specific instruction based on students' needs.

When unaccompanied by models, rubrics may not fully convey what we want students to do. On the other hand, when teachers systematically use rubrics with accompanying exemplars and anchor papers,[1] they find an overall increase in students' performance. This increase results in the welcomed situation of having to raise the standards for subsequent generations of students.

Examples of Rubrics   Some of the following examples of rubrics are associated with the tasks described previously in this chapter.

---

1. *Exemplars* are models that depict the highest standard for students' performances. *Anchors* are examples of performance for the intermediate levels of a rubric or scale.

Analytic Rubric for a Story Written by First Graders in
Lorianne Perrelle and Jane Lemak's Classes

	One	Two	Three	Four
Picture	"Simple" picture	"Good" picture	Very good picture that goes with the story	Great picture that goes with the story and adds detail
Readability	Author cannot read the story	Only the author can read the story	Someone else can read parts of the story with help from the author	Someone else can read the story
Focus	Does not tell a story	Tells a story	Tells a whole story, but not with complete sentences	Two or more complete sentences that tell a whole story
Use of conventions	Does not use capitals, periods, and question marks	Tries to use capitals, periods, and question marks	Sometimes uses correct capitals, periods, and questions marks	Uses correct capitals, periods, and question marks

This rubric shows that first graders are expected to have a solid grasp of some of the critical components of a good picture story: illustrations, focus, readability, and use of conventions. However, without exemplars and anchors, it would be difficult to truly agree on the specific meaning of some of the rubric descriptors, such as " 'good' picture."

The following holistic rubric from Barbara Vertucci's fifth-grade class is for a persuasive letter to the principal:

3   The request is reasonable and attainable; the reader understands the nature of the request and the reasons supporting it; and the reader agrees with the writer's rationale and considers and (if possible) takes action in favor of the request.

2   The request is reasonable in theory but is not necessarily attainable due to circumstances beyond the student's control (for example, placing lockers in the hallway may be reasonable but fire laws get in the way); the reader isn't exactly sure of what she is being persuaded to agree with or do; the student needs to be more specific by adding some examples or details or by finding more precise vocabulary; the reader is not completely convinced about what the student wants or why she wants it.

1   The request is unreasonable or unattainable (for example, asking for candy for breakfast every day); the reader does not understand what the student wants; more information and examples are needed to make the request clear; the reader would refuse to agree with the student given the request and its reasons.

Even though this rubric ignores conventional writing dimensions such as organization and mechanics, it succeeds in characterizing the intrinsic qualities of a good persuasive argument. It also calls attention to the inherent relationship between a writer's intent and a reader's response.

The following holistic rubric is for a tenth-grade summer reading project in Jim Quinn's class. Students must develop an artistic project that embodies their understanding of a book they have read.

5   The artistic response is distinctly original, showing exceptional insight into the work read. Demonstration of an understanding of character whose voice is assumed is clearly apparent. The link between the character and the book stimulates the viewer to new thought.

4   The student has selected an aspect about the work that is valid for the piece of literature read. The product clearly explores theme, action, setting, or symbol in a thoughtful, organized manner. The response accurately depicts the character from the work studied in class as it communicates a valid understanding and interpretation of the work studied.

3   Specific references to the actions, words, and thoughts of the character in the required work demonstrate the reader's interaction with some aspect of the work read independently. An organizing idea about the work is evident, showing that the reader understood it. The response will enable those who view it to become interested enough in the work of literature to read and talk about it.

2   The response does not appear to be complete or polished enough. It is not clear in organization or focus; the audience has difficulty in determining the writer/artist's intent. More thought about the piece of literature seems to be needed to communicate something valid about the work.

1   The product does not communicate the reader's understanding of the work of literature. Inaccuracies or irrelevancies are evident. The linkage between the work read and the artistic project seems to have been hastily undertaken, or the product may reveal only a plot summary rather than an analysis of both the characters and the work.

Jim Quinn's rubric is noteworthy because it establishes a relationship between creative work and literary insight and it provides students with an avenue to demonstrate their understanding and insights from material read outside class.

Exemplars

Exemplars are models that can be used by teachers and students to depict desired attributes of quality in products and performances. These models embody standards and scoring criteria that provide teachers and students with powerful images and pictures of high-quality work. If used systematically throughout the instructional process, exemplars can guide students' thinking, planning, development, and performance.

Teachers need to use multiple and varied exemplars to provide students with opportunities to internalize attributes of quality rather than to perceive the work to be done as driven by a formula. If students only use one or two exemplars, they often treat these exemplars as recipes and copy them. Therefore, teachers should show students at least three exemplars that depict very different approaches to producing quality work. In addition, teachers should draw from three different kinds of exemplars: one produced by students in the same grade level; one produced by students in subsequent grade levels and/or in schools that represent a higher educational level; and one produced by people outside schools in the context of engaging with authentic experiences (e.g., professional published work, commercial brochures, political debates, public performances, etc.).

A significant problem in using and interpreting exemplars produced in school lies in documenting the extent to which they were produced independently by the students or scaffolded or supported by the teacher or by others. Producing an exemplary product alone within time constraints is not the same task as producing an exemplary product with a significant amount of coaching, scaffolding, or unlimited time. This situation often prevails if a teacher is working with a special needs population where assistance is appropriately provided or time limits are eliminated. Therefore, it is important for teachers to annotate exemplars by describing the contextual and support-related factors that led to their creation. Some constraints are more important than others. Therefore, it is important for teachers to annotate exemplars by describing the contextual and support-related factors that led to their creation. As long as the teacher documents the kind of special circumstance that occurred (e.g., the student dictated the story to an aide, or the student did the task untimed), the exemplar is still valid.

Reconciling

To reconcile the use of standards, performance criteria, and expectations, we need to summarize the distinctions between the terms. *Criteria* refer to the different conditions that performances or products must meet to be considered of high quality. *Standards* are set once the task or process and its appropriate criteria are established. Standards characterize exemplary performance. Exemplars depict standards. Standards are not the same as expectations. *Expectations* refer to what we hope for and believe students should produce. It is very possible that no student will reach the standards for a given performance or product on a given grade. However, this does not mean we should not use the standards as a means to "stretch" our students. The goal is to assist students in improving their individual performance through self-analysis and understanding of what successful products look like rather than to foster unhealthy competition or to set unrealistic and unattainable goals. Students' sincere efforts to meet desired standards of quality need to be acknowledged, even if they have not yet met with success.

Teachers must decide how to translate their standards into expectations in terms of grades. For some rubrics, it is possible to have a one-to-one correspondence between the rubric and the grade; for others, the conversion might entail equating a lower point on the rubric to the top grade. Nonetheless, reconciling assessments and grades requires much more than technical solutions. In essence, grading is a normative process informed as much by political and philosophical issues as by technical concerns. As individuals, teachers can legitimize their grading criteria by making it explicit at the beginning of the year. To do this, they need to consider the specific factors that comprise students' grades. For example, to the extent that teachers incorporate effort (perseverance through revision) and progress as well as achievement into students' grades, they should determine the percentage of the grade that these factors encompass. They should also identify the specific evidence they will associate with these factors. Once defined, the weighing and evidence attached to these factors should be stable and consistent for all students.

However, there are limits to what individual teachers can do to rationalize their grading practices. Reconciling assessments with grades is as difficult as coming to terms with the dual roles that teachers need to play in the classroom; teachers must act as coaches and judges. Rational and equitable grading and reporting mechanisms can only be defined after having substantive conversations among students, parents, teachers, administrative staff, and policy members regarding the use and value of grades and report cards. These conversations need to be based on a shared definition of learner outcomes and performance standards with accompanying representative student work. Asking hard questions about these issues should be at the heart of professional development programs that recognize and respect the inherent complexities of education.

4

Seeing Our Growth as Learners
The Story of a First-Grade Teacher and Her Students

Rebecca Collins
edited by Diane Cunningham

The magic of portfolio assessment at the primary level is the
continuous opportunity for students to see their growth.
Rebecca Collins

*Rebecca Collins is a first-grade teacher at Church Street School
in White Plains, New York. She has a master's degree in Early
Childhood Education and has been a teacher at the primary level
for twelve years. Since completing the Hudson Valley Portfolio
Assessment Project, Rebecca continues to use portfolio assessment
with first graders. While the direction of her portfolio changes from
year to year, student reflection remains a constant element.
Rebecca believes that reflection is the most effective means of
getting young children to self assess and set goals. Rebecca shares
her learning by presenting workshops on the development
of performance tasks and, more recently, on parent involvement.
She is currently seeking certification in administration
and supervision from the State University of New York
at New Paltz, where she is focusing on staff development.*

*This chapter highlights a shift in position that is at the heart of the
journeys of many teachers in the Hudson Valley Project. As Rebecca
Collins explored portfolio assessment over three years she changed*

from a teacher who viewed assessment as solely her responsibility and something to be done for the report card, to a teacher who views assessment as both the students' and the teacher's responsibility. Assessment is no longer separate from her curriculum and instruction. Rather it has become an integral part of the learning opportunities that she provides for her first graders.

My transformation from wondering how I might use portfolios in a first-grade classroom, where many students begin the year unable to read and write, to believing that portfolios are one of the most effective methods of helping first graders develop as readers and writers, began when I became a member of the Hudson Valley Portfolio Assessment Project. The change in my thinking and practice has been as dramatic as the change in my first-grade students, who move from saying "I can't read that story" and "I don't know how to write" to students who see themselves as readers and writers and recognize the progress they've made.

Even though I was one of just a few primary-level teachers in the project and I questioned what my role would be in portfolio development, I felt part of a grassroots movement of assessment design and reform. My participation allowed me to see what portfolio assessment looks like at all levels, K–12. I saw that students in all grades were being asked to select work, reflect on it, evaluate it, and set goals. I saw that my design could play a crucial role for my students' future learning and involvement with portfolios.

Over time, I came to see that the magic of portfolio assessment at the primary level is the continuous opportunity for students to see their growth. This was critical for me. When I started in the project, I believed that I would help my students see themselves as readers and writers by showing them how much they'd improved. Now, I strongly believe that the transformation from "I can't" to "I can" occurs when *students* show *themselves* how they've improved.

Before I became involved in the project, I knew little about portfolios and their benefits for students' learning. My expectations of students and of their abilities to self-assess were too low. The purpose of assessment in my classroom was to determine what I should put on the report card, not to help my students become aware of themselves as learners and to assess themselves. It never occurred to me to have *students* see their work for purposes of evaluation, to show them what an exemplary piece of work looked like, or to provide them with a rubric they could use to evaluate their work. I thought the students would *figure out* what was expected and why they got the grades they received.

The Hudson Valley Project helped me to see that I have the expertise and knowledge to design appropriate assessment tools for my classroom and, more important, that it would take time for me to change my assessment practices. Assignments, lessons, and assessment tools had to be created, used, amended, and revised before the portfolio became a valid assessment for my students. My design evolved as a result of what I saw children do with their portfolios over the three years that I worked in the project. As I observed and listened to students I moved from thinking of portfolios as a collection of work to thinking of portfolios as a vehicle for student learning. I gained a truer understanding of the potential for learning that portfolio assessment can provide for students, parents, and teachers.

Setting the Stage for Portfolios in a First-Grade Classroom

Helping Students Move from "I Can't" to "I Can"

My first question at the start of every year is How will I ensure that the students make a shift from feeling that they can't read and write to feeling that they can? I believe that a student's attitude about learning has to be a primary focus in first grade. In most cases the biggest barriers that confront first graders are their lack of confidence and a fear of making mistakes. On the whole, they hesitate and question before taking the risks that learners need to take. For example, on the day I introduce my students to Writer's Workshop and Reader's Workshop, they voice their beliefs that they can't read and write. Like falling dominoes, one student after another says, "But I can't do this, I don't know how to write!" Or, "I can't read *that* story, I can't read." Or, "How do you spell . . . I can't spell." Their voices echo throughout the classroom.

Each September, I face a variety of skill levels and attitudes. Each of my students reacts differently to the first assignment, to write about something they did during the summer. One student, Howard, spent the entire time talking to other children, getting up and down to ask me to help him, and along the way becoming so disruptive that other children at his table were unable to work. Another child, Nathalie, just sat at her seat crying because I wouldn't tell her how to spell every word. Harry, a confident student, simply went ahead to write his story.

This first piece of writing serves as a baseline sample. I learned in the project that if I want the portfolio to document my students' growth in reading and writing, it must contain baseline information about their abilities. And, since I am sure that their attitudes are critical to their development, I also need baseline information about their perceptions and feelings about themselves as readers and writers. So, in addition to taking an early writing and reading sample, I ask students questions about themselves, such as:

How do you feel when you are reading?

Are you a reader?

How do you know?

As the children develop, the baselines give us something to compare to each step of the way. My students' abilities to see and understand growth come when I help them notice the specific ways in which their work is changing. This modeling is one key to the success of portfolios in my classroom. At the start, I point out to them how their skills are developing: "Remember the first day of school how you wrote your name? Now look at the letters." Or, "Look at the first story you wrote. How is that story different from this story?" Invariably the smiles appear as they begin to notice the differences.

Modeling the Right Mind-Set

Because many of my students are driven by perfection and are afraid to try something new for fear they might fail, I use many of my own stories about my learning experiences to point out that making mistakes and taking chances are a part of learning. Specifically, I like to tell them about my sewing. I bring in projects I'm doing and share my mistakes and my triumphs. They see my willingness to try, my successes, and my failures. Above all, they see the work that goes into learning and the rewards that can result. As I model this mind-set, I have the children write and read whenever possible so they can also take some risks. I encourage them to try. Mistakes become the norm and learning tools for future understanding. We applaud approximation and acknowledge our effort.

Providing Instruction and Practice in Writing

Part of preparing first-grade students to be successful in using a portfolio involves direct instruction of the mechanics and strategies of reading and writing. I have to help students to improve their work by reviewing the sound/symbol relationship, punctuation, finger spacing, and handwriting so they can incorporate these skills into their reading and writing. I comfortably incorporate these lessons into shared book time or mini-lessons taught in the context of real literature. As the children begin to use the conventions of print in their work and as I provide opportunities for them to publish some of their books, they begin to feel like real authors.

While students are learning about conventions we also have discussions about the various strategies that readers and writers use. I ask them questions such as:

What strategies will help you to communicate your thoughts on paper?

What strategies can you use to figure out a word you don't know?

What strategies can you use to add more detail and organize your story?

In our discussions, students learn about reading strategies that include:

Predict what word would make sense.

Look at the illustration to predict what words you might read.

Skip a word you don't know and reread the sentence.

Predict what you think will happen at the end.

These strategies are not only useful for improving reading skills but also provide children with the necessary language for verbalizing how they have developed as readers. Our discussions give students a foundation from which to draw when they evaluate their own work. For example, when Harry is writing about how he has improved as a reader, he is able to express his abilities with the vocabulary he has learned (Figure 4–1).

Figure 4–1
Harry's Reflection on His Reading

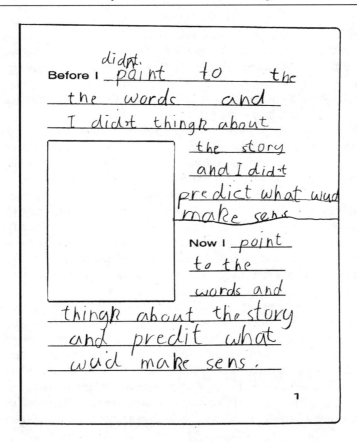

We also have discussions about the behaviors of readers and writers. Students won't know what writers and readers do if they have not been shown. I often role-play the part of a student who is displaying the appropriate behaviors of a writer or reader during workshop time. We then list the things I am doing correctly or incorrectly. The children enjoy being the evaluators, perhaps because they can see themselves in what I am doing: writing many sentences, thinking about my writing, sounding out words, and making illustrations to go with my story. In addition, the learning that occurs in these discussions lays a foundation for developing reading and writing rubrics with the children.

Using Rubrics and Exemplars

Once I get students reading, writing, and thinking about what they do, I must consider the next questions:

How will students know what a "good" piece of work looks like?

How will they decide which items should go into the portfolio?

As I participated in the Hudson Valley Project, I learned about the value of rubrics and exemplars for students. At first, I was not immediately sure about how and when to best introduce these to my first graders. This was new territory for me. But I knew that using these tools could bring my students' ability to self-evaluate and reflect on their learning to higher levels. So, I started by showing the children student work from previous years and then guiding my students in critiquing them.

Now as a first step toward developing rubrics, my students and I review work together to decide how we can tell when a piece of writing is good or how we know that a story has substance. It takes practice for my students to learn how to describe what they see. Through teacher and student modeling, practice, and discussion, the students begin to "get it," verbalizing things like "The illustration is very detailed." "The writer used words that made pictures in your head." "This story did not have a main character." It is satisfying to hear my six- and seven-year-old students talk about books and stories in such a mature fashion. Their vocabulary is much richer than I remember from my past teaching experiences. Even parents remark about how impressed they are with their children's understanding and love of books.

After having exposed the children to exemplary student work, much good literature, and strategies and behaviors, I move to discussions about rubrics. Because students have been through the process of describing what a reader and writer looks like and does, they are quite capable of working with me in developing an expectation guide, or rubric. The checklist in Figure 4–2 is the first step toward developing a rubric. These checklists and rubrics are an important outgrowth of their learning. Because we have identified criteria, students have a basis for selection when choosing pieces for their portfolios.

Figure 4–2
Student Self-Evaluation of Writing Sample

Student Self-Evaluation of Writing Sample

Name _____

A writer...

...writes many sentences.

...writes words to tell a story.

...thinks about what she/he wants to write about.

...sounds words out to hear all the sounds

...makes illustrations to go with his/her words.

...decides if she/he is finished with the story.

I was a writer because _____

_____

This is how I felt about my writing.

3 ☺   2 ☺   1 ☹
great   okay   I could do better

My writing will be even better if I _____

The Portfolio at Work in a First-Grade Classroom

From the very first day of school, a portfolio box is always visible. Initially I have brief conversations with the children about what the box is for, but when I give them a formal introduction to the portfolio box, I talk to them about how this will be a place to keep work that shows us what they're doing as readers and writers. I also inform them that they will select most of the work that goes into the portfolio and that sometimes I will ask them to put a piece in. To get an idea of their understanding of the portfolio, I have them write about it. In my first year of the project, I had them write about the portfolio early in the year. The children echoed my comments and consistently wrote that this is a place to keep their best work. The next year I had the children write about portfolios later in the year. Daniel's piece is shown in Figure 4–3. I never would have thought that a six-year-old could verbalize such depth of thinking had I not used a portfolio. This was further compelling evidence that made me ask, How could I not use a portfolio?

My students are free to make selections for their portfolio whenever they

Figure 4–3
Daniel's Reflection on Portfolios

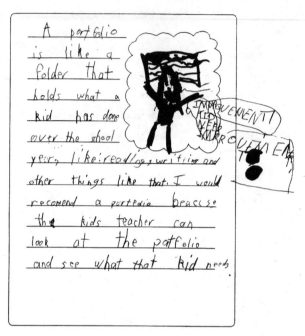

A portfolio is like a folder that holds what a kid has done over the school year, like: reading, writing and other things like that. I would recomend a portfolio beaccse the kids teacher can look at the patfolio and see what that kid needs

improrvement on and what thy are verry good at. So... Por-tfolio time! Portfolio time! Time to get youre GREAT, EXELENT, portfolio today!

want. When I began, I feared that the portfolio would end up with *all* of their work, but as they matured they became more discerning. The fact that they must also complete an entry form makes them more selective. The only time I get involved is prior to report cards when I specifically want to make sure key elements are included. By allowing students to have most of the control of the portfolio, I have more time to observe what they do and to guide their use of the portfolio.

As students make selections they become critical—sometimes too critical—about how they fare on the rating sheet. As I meet with them, I ask them to set goals for future writing. Some of their goals include:

Next time I will make sure the pictures connect with the words.

Next time I will add more words.

Next time I will make my illustrations more detailed.

As students go through the conferencing process, they develop a more objective approach to looking at their work. Our conferences empower them to be part of the assessment/evaluation procedure, so when they receive their report card or their parents come home from parent-teacher conferences with specific comments, the children are not surprised. They are much more aware of what they know and what they need to learn next.

Educating Parents Through Portfolios

Before I prepare report cards, I also ask students to complete another reflection to get a pulse on how they are feeling about themselves as writers and readers. It acts as a powerful tool to share with parents during conferences. Parents, with good intentions, often put pressure on their children to be perfect. I sometimes hear, "I can't work with my child because she doesn't know how to spell all those words or doesn't know how to read the story so I get angry." These parents need guidance in how to work with their children or they may destroy all I have done to build confidence and encourage risk taking in the classroom. The portfolio allows me to show parents a reflection of their children's learning. I can be specific about growth and parents begin to understand their children's developmental journeys. It has been my experience that parents, when shown, can begin to understand that learning takes time and practice. When I share the students' reflection pieces, the parents can then see the connection between how their children feel about themselves and what they produce.

The Value of Portfolio Assessment: Nathalie's Story

As I designed and experimented with portfolio assessment in my classroom, it was important for me to keep an ongoing dialogue with some students to understand how they were perceiving and using portfolios. I followed Nathalie closely because she personified "I can't." She came to first grade knowing all of the letters but not all of the sounds, and she had a few words in her writing and reading repertoire but little experience in the writing or reading process. When it was time to write, she would say that she didn't know how to write. She often ended up in tears because I would not give her spellings for the words that she wanted to use. She was a little more willing to read, but she was always guarded about making mistakes and did not push herself beyond what she already knew. She seemed almost ashamed of her abilities.

On her attitude survey she consistently filled in the "Not So Good" face, and her response would be that she didn't know how to write or read. When asked if she was a writer or reader she would respond, "No!" because she didn't know many words.

By the middle of the year, however, her simplistic responses were no longer present. When asked how she felt when she was writing or reading, she indicated, "Great!" When asked why, she explained that she was now able to read many books. She often chose books to read and stated that she liked certain authors. She beamed when she said that her mother was so proud of what she knew. Nathalie wrote in an end-of-the-year reflection form some of the ways she had improved in reading (Figure 4–4).

As she considered her writing, Nathalie stated, "Now that I read so many different words I know them when I need them in my stories." She also said, "I write such long stories now and my pictures are so detailed."

Nathalie learned to look at her work objectively and to point out specific ways she had improved. She moved from a simple stage of writing and thinking—"I like my friend, she is fun,"—to more complex stories incorporating what she was learning and stories she had heard. She developed her own talent and wrote the following story, incorporating the style of a book I had read to the class into her own work:

Do you like the snow?
Do you like to watch the snow fall?
Do you like to make a snowman?
Do you like to make a snow fort?
     Do you?
     I do.

She told me that she liked thinking of ways to make her stories a little different. I heard her provide a suggestion to a child who was writing about colors: "Rather than just write a color on each page, why don't you ask a question? That way your story will be more interesting. Like, 'What is red?' Then you can write down some things that are red. That will make your story a little different."

When I had a discussion with Nathalie about how she had grown as a learner, she laughed about how she used to be. She was so removed from that girl who used to cry. When I asked her to tell me some ways she had changed, she said:

Figure 4–4
Nathalie's Reflection on Her Reading

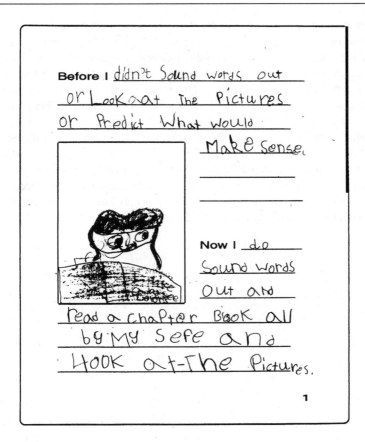

Before I didn't Sound words out or Look at The Pictures or Predict What would Make Sense.

_____

_____

Now I do Sound words out and read a chapter Book all by my sefe and Look at The Pictures.

1

Well, I know I really work hard now. I even write at home so I can do better. When I write stories I like to do something different, that makes it more interesting. Now that I read I use those words to help me write. I know some words now so I can read easy and hard books. When I don't know a word I sound it out, I make the sounds the letters make.

"How do you know you're learning?" I asked. She pulled some papers out of her portfolio and said, "One thing I do now is make my letters smaller. See, my _h_ used to look like an _n_. Also, my stories are much longer now. See how my pictures have more _detail?_"

When I reminded her about how she always had to get things right, she laughed and said, "It doesn't matter if you're wrong or right, the most important thing is that I'm learning. You know how people say you learn from mistakes."

Clearly, Nathalie delights in her growth and enjoys writing. At the end of the year Nathalie was the proud author of two books, one fiction and the other nonfiction.

Prior to my involvement in the project, I would not have given Nathalie the time or opportunity to review her work, notice her progress, and learn about what she can do. The portfolio I developed allowed her to track her progress and see for herself the strides she made. In a November reading response reflection sheet she wrote, "[This story was too hard] cas I do no ho to rir [because I do not know how to read]." Later she wrote, "This story was just right because I could read all the words. I could sound them all out." Nathalie speaks with a specificity and knowledge of herself as a learner that confirms, for me, the value of portfolio assessment. Her dramatic transformation from a student who personified "I can't" to a student who can articulate her strengths and weaknesses mirrors the transformation I experienced. Over three years, I've moved from wondering, How can I use portfolio assessment in a first-grade classroom? to asserting, How can I not?

5

Helping Children Monitor Their Own Learning

Robin Sostak
edited by Diana Muxworthy Feige

I was certain that this group of students could never put together a quality, substantive rubric. . . . We began by listing the qualities of great poetry. I was in shock! What they brainstormed were the exact qualities I would have identified.

Robin Sostak

Robin Sostak is a sixth-grade language arts and math teacher in Liberty Middle School, Sullivan County, New York, a school in which teams of teachers play a strong leadership role in implementing new curricula and assessments. She has been teaching for eleven years, five as a first-grade teacher and six as a sixth-grade teacher. Throughout her teaching career, she has studied and followed the writing process philosophy and format of Lucy Calkins' Writing Project at Teacher's College. During the three years of the Hudson Valley Project she designed language arts and math portfolios. The language arts portfolio, primarily because of her reduced number of students (twenty-five), was the sole source of the students' final grade. Because she had fifty math students, the problem-solving portfolio was completed twice a year and was not graded.

Giving students the tools to self-reflect, ponder, and direct their own development, Robin Sostak rediscovered her role as a teacher. The more she improved those tools, the more the students surprised her in their willingness and ability to direct their

*learning. Open-ended queries invited self-reflection; the
collaborative process of designing meaningful rubrics then
crystallized the merits of this reflection and was the key to
three incarnations of portfolios that ultimately led to Robin's
wholehearted commitment to student ownership of their learning.*

*Diana Muxworthy Feige is Director of School-Based Programs
in the School of Education at Adelphi University in Garden City,
New York. In that capacity, many of her efforts are dedicated
to deepening partnerships between secondary schools and
teacher education programs. She supervises teaching interns
(primarily in English Language Arts classrooms) and teaches
foundations as well as curriculum and instruction courses for
pre-service and in-service students. Until recently, she served
as the Associate Editor of the* Holistic Education Review,
*working closely with educators committed to re-envisioning authentic,
meaning-rich learning environments. Diana
completed her doctoral studies in the Department of Family
and Community Education at Teachers College,
Columbia University, following completion of a
master's degree at Harvard Divinity School.*

I am a very different teacher now than I was three years ago. Three years
ago, I could not have imagined how I would evolve as a teacher. I could
not have imagined the quality of work my students now produce. I could
not have imagined their thoughtfulness, reflection, and understanding. I
could not have imagined the overwhelming transformation that my own
thinking and teaching would undergo as I implemented portfolios in my
classroom.

I greeted the Hudson Valley Project assuming I would learn about the
new buzz words in education and be able to bring something back to improve my teaching. Never did I realize what a tremendous metamorphosis it
would yield. Two questions, covert at first, became my fulcrum, the pivot
upon which all would turn. I struggled through these questions for three
years: Can students truly be responsible enough to take ownership and ultimate control of their own learning? Can I trust them to direct their learning?
In the beginning, my answer would have been a resounding no. I would
have said that it is the teacher's job to take control of the learning that oc-

curs in the classroom. I felt that if I gave my students too much control, they would accomplish less and produce inferior work. I can't believe how wrong I was.

Composing Rubrics: The Transformation Begins

By the end of the Hudson Valley Project's first summer session, I had established my outcomes and indicators. The effort was not too tasking, and it was clearly worthwhile. The next rite of passage, which is what each task felt like, was identifying criteria for my first-ever rubric. I met with my language arts teammate, Terry Planica, to discuss ways of making our grades more consistent. Rubrics were our key to that commitment.

Terry and I looked at other rubrics and shared what we felt was good writing. This discussion was immensely fruitful. In our combined twenty years of teaching, neither of us had ever identified what we saw in good writing. Our four established categories were focus/organization, development, language, and mechanics (Figure 5–1). The language we used in our rubric was unmistakably teacher-directed. I didn't recognize that at the time, and I proceeded with eager anticipation.

More precisely, I stormed the classroom. I was exhilarated, confident that I was opening doors for them because for the first time I was letting them know clearly and specifically what was expected of them. I anticipated that their work and effort would improve in leaps and bounds.

The students went to work setting goals for themselves as writers, discussing what constitutes good writing. I introduced the rubric with the intent of letting them know upfront how I planned to assess their work. In math, I taught problem-solving strategies and invited the students to solve problems a couple times a week. I showed them what I felt were important attributes of exemplary problem solving. Then I introduced the rubric (Figure 5–2) and expected the kids to use it.

By the end of September, I was thrilled. I had never before, at this early juncture in the school year, done such a thorough job of assessing where the students were academically. Based on that assessment, I knew exactly what I needed to teach. I loved the precision of the evaluations and the clarity of direction.

Looking back, I recognize that at this point in my professional development, the focus was entirely on me. I saw myself as the sole assessor. My goals were to illuminate my criteria so that the students would strive to achieve more, and to use my criteria so that I would be more consistent as an evaluator. Terry and I were also, at long last, grading more consistently between classes. I was more than content.

My bliss, however, was short lived. Around October, I woke up to the fact that the language of both the math and writing rubrics was not accessible

Figure 5–1
Writing Rubric, Draft 1

	Focus/Organization	Development
4	• Clear topic • Logical progression of ideas • No digressions • Clear sense of beginning and ending	• Elements of narrative developed well (plot, setting, characters, etc.) • Ideas fully supported • Details vivid and specific
3	• Clear topic • Most events logical • Some digressions causing slight reader distraction • Limited sense of beginning and ending	• Elements present but lack depth • Some ideas supported • Details present but not specific
2	• Topic may not be clear • Few events are logical • Much digression or elaboration with significant interference to reader • Little sense of beginning and ending	• Elements not evenly developed (some may be omitted) • Minimal support of ideas • Details may be irrelevant or confusing
1	• Topic is not clear • No clear organization • No attempt to limit topic • Almost no sense of beginning and ending	• Little development of narrative elements • No support of ideas • No details
0	• Totally unrelated to the topic • Illegible • Incoherent (words make no sense)	

Figure 5–1
Continued

Language	**Mechanics**
4 • Shows skillful use of sentence variety • Specific and vivid language	• Little development of narrative • Few or no mechanical errors
3 • Some sentence variety • Appropriate use of language	• Mechanical errors that do not interfere with communication
2 • Shows some sentence sense but no variety (uses simple sentences) • Occasionally uses inappropriate or incorrect language	• Mechanical errors that interfere with communication
1 • Sentences do not make sense • Frequently uses inappropriate or incorrect language	• Mechanical errors that make communication very difficult

Figure 5–2
Weekly Problem Rubric, Draft 1

Exemplary **Response = 5**

- Demonstrates understanding of problem through clear explanation of task
- Effectively communicates thinking process
- Uses clear, coherent, unambiguous, and elegant explanations
- Shows evidence of reflection on solution (the answer makes sense)
- Includes examples and strong supporting arguments

Competent **Response = 4**

- Provides a fairly complete response with reasonably clear explanations
- Communicates thinking process
- Shows an understanding of problem
- Presents supporting arguments

Satisfactory **= 3**

- Completes the problem satisfactorily but explanation may be muddled
- May not provide complete articulation of problem
- May not use appropriate examples or diagrams of thinking process
- Understands underlying mathematical ideas

Serious Flaws **= 2**

- Begins the problem appropriately but may fail to complete or may omit significant parts of the problem
- May fail to show full understanding of mathematical ideas and processes
- May make major computational errors
- May reflect an inappropriate strategy for solving the problem

Inadequate **Response = 1**

- Is unable to begin effectively
- Uses words that do not reflect the problem
- Fails to indicate which information is appropriate

NO ATTEMPT **= 0**

Figure 5–3
Writing Rubric, Draft 2

4   An *excellent* writing piece:

Focus/Organization	• Establishes and maintains a clear purpose
	• Organizes ideas in a logical way
Development	• Has a clear beginning that pulls readers into the story
	• Has an ending that ties loose parts of story together
	• Has ideas that are well supported with appropriate details
Language	• Uses vivid, specific, and interesting language
	• Uses language that flows
Mechanics	• Mistakes in grammar, mechanics, and usage are minimal or nonexistent and do not interfere with enjoyment of the story

3   A *good* writing piece:

Focus/Organization	• Maintains a purpose
	• Uses logical organization, may include some digressions
Development	• Provides some details to clarify ideas
	• Has a limited sense of beginning and ending
Language	• Attempts to use interesting language
	• Uses transitions that may be choppy
Mechanics	• Mistakes in grammar, mechanics, and usage do not interfere with enjoyment of the story

2   A *fair* writing piece:

Focus/Organization	• Has some awareness of purpose
	• Attempts to organize ideas, includes much digression or elaboration that interferes with the story
Development	• Has minimal support of ideas
	• Includes some details that may be irrelevant or confusing
Language	• Uses simple sentences, no variety
	• Uses little or no interesting language
Mechanics	• Mistakes may interfere with enjoyment of the story

1   An *unsatisfactory* writing piece:

Focus/Organization	• Is confused in purpose, no limit to topic
	• Has no clear organization
Development	• Uses few or no details
	• Has little or no sense of beginning and ending
Language	• Includes sentences that do not make sense
	• Frequently uses inappropriate or incorrect language
Mechanics	• Mistakes seriously interfere with communication

to the students. It was too difficult, too out of reach. Besides that, the organization of the writing rubric was confusing; the students didn't understand it.

The bubble burst, and the first of many revisions followed. Terry and I went back to the drawing board. We were, one way or another, going to get "this rubric thing" right. We liked the four established categories in the language arts rubric. They were comprehensive and useful, so we decided to keep them. We added, though, descriptors to flesh out the picture of excellent writing. We used language we thought would be more accessible. We reorganized the four categories to *follow* each descriptor (Figure 5–3).

The students responded favorably to this new writing rubric. Together, we entered a new chapter in our travels. They began to make intentional revisions based on the rubric; in short, they began to take control of their writing. I hadn't experienced this before, ever. I had always been the boss in charge of grading their work. They had done what they thought was their best and the rest had been in my hands. I had had full control over the grade, without sharing my criteria for evaluation with them. In fact, I simply had been grading on a feeling, an impression of how their work sounded as I read it. Now we both had understandable, usable criteria. They knew what I wanted, and I knew what I wanted.

Composing Portfolios: An Awakening

The creation of portfolios invited me—no, forced me—to keep rethinking and revising the rubrics. The first portfolio, which accompanied the first marking period's report cards, was meager and, as with the rubrics, very teacher directed. I told students what to do and they did it. They chose four pieces to include in the portfolios; they completed the self-reflection (Figure 5–4); they answered the three given questions about their best and worst work and about themselves as writers (Figure 5–5); they looked at the goals they set for themselves, explained how they worked to meet them, and set new goals for the next marking period; and they completed a cover letter to tie it all together (Figure 5–6).

Even with this meager portfolio, I saw better work than I had in the past. Students were more excited than they had ever been in my class. They were thrilled about what they had accomplished. We were flying high. I wrote in my log,

> I think the one thing that really surprised me about the portfolios is who benefited the most from them. I went into the year assuming I would know my writers better through their portfolios. What I discovered is that the kids were the ones who really were beginning to know themselves as writers. They were really evaluating themselves.

Figure 5–4
Student Self-Reflection

Student Name _____   Date _____

1. What makes a good piece of writing?

2. How have you used this information to improve your writing?

3. What strategies do you use before you begin a piece of writing?

4. What strategies do you use to revise a piece?

5. What do you do to edit a piece?

6. What part of writing is the hardest for you?

Figure 5–5
Best Piece Analysis

Student Name _____

Assignment Chosen _____

1. Why did you choose this piece for your portfolio?

_____

_____

_____

2. What decisions did you make that made this piece work

well?_____

_____

_____

_____

3. What did you learn about good writing by doing this

piece? _____

_____

_____

This was a revelation to me. I now wanted students to get more involved in their own assessment. They could do it; they ran with it. Although I had thought I was already making students responsible for their own work, with this first portfolio I realized that I had never given the students the tools to be responsible for and take ownership of their own learning. And yet without

Figure 5–6
Initial Portfolio Cover Letter

Date _____

Dear _____,

Here is my writing portfolio for this marking period. I would
like you to notice this about my work:

1. I have tried very hard to do

2. Something I still need to work on is

3. Something else I really want you to know about my work is

I hope you are proud of me.

Sincerely,

---

giving them opportunities to reflect on their learning and to know the specific
criteria for evaluation, how could I ever expect them truly to care and take responsibility for themselves as learners?

Reflection and self-evaluation became my new call to arms. I made two
shifts simultaneously in both the writing and problem-solving assessment. I
examined exemplary problem solving and writing, and then I revised the
rubrics so that we completed the assessment analytically rather than holisti-
cally (Figures 5–7 and 5–8). I assigned points to each criteria, and the students and I evaluated each separately and distinctly. I designed a weekly
problem-solving rubric and asked the students to self-evaluate based on each
criteria. The students responded positively; I saw an immediate improvement
in the quality of their work.

Figure 5–7
Weekly Problem Rubric, Draft 2

Understanding the Task (What do I know from the problem and what do I have to find out?)	0	No important information or question to be solved
	1	Part of information given
	2	Complete restatement of important information
Planning a Solution (How do I solve it?)	0	No attempt or an inappropriate plan or strategy
	1	Partially correct plan
	2	Plan could lead to correct solution if implemented correctly
Carrying Out Your Plan (What did I have to think about and decide to solve the problem?)	0	Did not tell what you did
	1	Gave some explanation, but not clear enough
	2	Clear explanation of all thinking done to solve the problem
Getting an Answer (Is my answer correct?)	0	No answer or answer not following a plan
	1	Computational error, partial error, or correct answer to incorrect plan
	2	Correct answer
Appearance (What does my piece look like?)	0	Unorganized and shows little effort
	1	Some organization, but not very neat
	2	Very organized and neatly done

Enthused by the success of the revised math rubric and added self-evaluation, Terry and I redesigned the writing rubric so that it was scored analytically and included an invitation for reflection and self-evaluation (Figure 5–9). The students evaluated their accomplishments according to each specified criteria. Based on that self-evaluation, they reflected on their successes and what they felt needed improvement. Quickly, they began to assimilate the characteristics of good writing. Continuously, they surpassed my expectations. I was one very happy teacher.

Figure 5–8
Writing Rubric, Draft 3

> Use this standard to
> evaluate each piece of writing in the following areas.
> **1 = well done   .5 = fair   0 = unsatisfactory**

Focus/Organization

* Establishes and maintains a clear purpose
* Stays on topic (focused)
* Uses logical organization (sequential, orderly)
* Provides content that makes sense
* Is aware of audience

Development

* Has a clear beginning (lead) that pulls readers into the story
* Has an ending that ties loose parts of the story together
* Includes ideas that are well supported with appropriate details
* Provides details and facts that are vivid and specific
* Shows imagination and creativity
* Allows the reader to feel, hear, and see the action (setting, characters, plot)
* Limits paragraphs to deal with one subject

Language

* Uses vivid, specific, and interesting language
* Uses fluent, clear, and appropriate language
* Uses sentence variety
* Uses a personal style (imagination and creativity)

Mechanics

* Includes proper grammar and usage
* Includes proper sentence construction
* Includes correct punctuation
* Includes correct capitalization
* Includes correct spelling

Figure 5–9
Writing Rubric, Draft 4

Title of Piece _____

Name of Author _____

Date _____

Assign a score for each category:
4 = excellent; 3 = good; 2 = fair; 1 = unsatisfactory

Characteristics of writing	Rating
Focus/Organization • Establishes and maintains a clear purpose • Uses logical organization	1 2 3 4
Development • Includes a strong beginning and ending • Shows development of ideas • Limits paragraphs to deal with one subject	1 2 3 4
Language • Uses vivid, specific, and interesting language • Uses fluent and clear language	1 2 3 4
Mechanics • Uses proper grammar • Uses proper sentence construction • Uses correct punctuation • Uses correct capitalization	1 2 3 4

What I did well _____

_____

_____

What I could have done better _____

_____

_____

Composing a Poetry Unit: Another Wake-Up Call

Often the most enlightening moments in teaching are the unexpected—the unplanned lesson serendipidously thrown to the students because there was absolutely no time to plan otherwise. Such was the case with the design of the rubric for a March poetry unit. It opened my eyes to the hidden, untapped resourcefulness of the children. It took me to seas I had never sailed.

The writing rubric that Terry and I had been using was not appropriate for evaluating poetry. Because I had no time to design a new rubric, I decided to do so in the writing workshop with the students. I hoped, and even assumed, that my best writers would volunteer. They didn't. Invited to collaboratively design the rubric, the only volunteers to come forward were a few generally unmotivated students who jumped at the opportunity to do something other than write—anything other than write. I resigned myself to going through the motions of brainstorming the rubric with this small group of volunteers, and then going home to write my own. I was certain that this group of students could never put together a quality, substantive rubric. They were, after all, the low achievers.

We began by listing the qualities of great poetry. I was in shock! What they brainstormed were the exact qualities I would have identified. I could not believe what I was seeing. Once we exhausted the list, we organized the criteria into categories: language, development and organization, and mechanics. I typed it up and presented it to the class the next day. Not only were the volunteers immediately proud of themselves, but they also were motivated to start writing poetry. They internalized the qualities of great poetry on a level I had not seen with the initial, more generic writing rubric. Their work improved dramatically. My sixth graders were becoming poets.

This was truly a humbling experience for me. I had assumed that an essential aspect of being a good writing teacher was to tell the students what made good writing. Now I found that students assimilated the information at a much higher level when they were involved in identifying the criteria. This blew open a new pattern of thinking for me. How could I get the children more involved in identifying criteria for their work? I wanted to provide this opportunity with everything I gave them but worried that time would be too scarce. After much internal debate, I decided that we would design rubrics together for the tasks that would be repeated often, such as ongoing writing and problem solving. I alone would design the rubrics for intermittent projects.

Composing Self-Reflection Queries: Less Is More

And so ended my first year of implementing portfolios and alternative assessments. We had emphasized the design of the rubrics. We had revised them three times, and they were now in the hands of the students to create. The students were self-evaluating their academic progress according to collaboratively established criteria. They were experiencing what it was to be

Figure 5–10
Portfolio "Prove It"

Writing Goals

Name _____   Marking Period _____

It is important to work consistently to improve ourselves as
writers. In doing this, you have set goals for yourself. We
want to see how you've used the information you have
learned about good writing to improve your own writing.

1. Identify the goals you have for improving your writing.

  1.

  2.

2. PROVE IT:

Look through your pieces of writing for this marking period
and explain how you worked to meet these goals. What did
you do in each piece? Use your teacher conference sheet to
help you. Give as much evidence to show improvement as
you can find.

  Goal 1:

  Goal 2:

---

self-reflective about their progress. But I still wanted to give students more
power over their learning. I wanted them to become more and more reflective about themselves as writers and problem solvers and, perhaps more
important, as learners. I wanted them to think about the decisions they
were making and why they were making them, to see themselves as learners, evolving and moving on. I wanted to see their thinking on paper and
understand them better as learners.

With this impetus, I added the "Prove It" section of the portfolios (Figure 5–10). We asked students to set writing goals and, using pieces of writing, to explore how they worked to achieve these goals and improve their writing. They started to pay more attention to their learning, to think about their thinking, and to document what they did and why they did it.

Before long, the bubble burst again. Over time, the students answered the various reflection invitations haphazardly. They were overdosing on reflection, and in response they were settling for a few casual words. Less is more became my operating rule. Or as Thoreau kept reminding us, Simplify. Simplify. Simplify. I cut the required number of self-selected best pieces from four to two and diminished what was becoming a bulky, perhaps somewhat redundant, portfolio. I asked the students to select two pieces and to invest time and effort in rigorous, thoughtful reflections about those selections. The streamlining worked and the reflections deepened; my workload evaluating the portfolios was reduced without sacrificing quality. Again, a simple but substantial revision—and more important, a change in my thinking, an awakening to quality over quantity, and a trusting of process and the children—made all the difference.

Composing New, Open-Ended Reflective Queries: Let the Fires Burn

In the midst of all this encouraging development, I was not completely satisfied. Some fundamental aspect of the portfolio needed reorientation. I was amazed by the students and their accomplishments, their willingness and ability to self-evaluate and to guide their own learning. In response, I wanted to get out of their way and let them run with the fire they were kindling inside.

The portfolio, as comprehensive and enticing as it was in its ability to mirror the children's thinking and progress, was not yet a full picture of who they were as writers. As primary designer of the portfolio, I was doing something that was stifling the texture and dimensionality of the picture. They knew more than they could communicate answering the limited questions I asked. They were more, and I was in their way.

I decided to lift the restraints: to replace directed, specific questions with a few open-ended questions that offered simple guidelines to stimulate reflection. At the end of the year I simply asked the students to compare themselves to the writers they were at the beginning of the year, using the portfolios to gather evidence, addressing their change, and discussing what they found easy and difficult. Again, the surprises didn't cease. The special education students, for example, communicated their growth differently from but as effectively as the "more able" students. Some students noted how writing helped them process their personal development, while others provided an analysis of their improvement in using the tools of writing:

Crystal's Response

In my writing process I have improved by really getting into my pieces and reading books then writing the information down and writing a story based on my work. I also have improved by going places and doing things and then writing about them. Sometimes they give me a really good idea to write a story.

I think writing is fun because you can learn a lot from what you write. For example, when I wrote Mr. Francisco, I learned that everybody has to let go of somebody sometime and that to get your words out of your head when you don't want to tell anyone about it, write it down in words and then you can get your feelings out. . . .

Oliver's Response

I think that I have greatly improved in writing since the beginning of the school year. Now when I write, I use dialogue, imagery, more interesting words and a lot more detail. For poetry, I try to and use white space well and to try to not force the rhyme. In fiction and essays I think my introductions and endings are crisp and exciting.

I think the portfolio has helped me a lot. It helps me understand the writing process a lot easier. It helped me improve in prewriting and editing tremendously. Even though it's a lot of work doing the reflections and stuff, but overall, its worth it because it makes me think more about writing than I ever have before. . . .

The students' reflections made me rethink the entire portfolio. I finally had a clear picture of what I wanted from them: I wanted students who could grow as writers and who could articulate their growth. During the second summer session of the Hudson Valley Project, I decided to take out the teacher restraints. The portfolio, now in its third incarnation, would include three pieces selected by the student for *any* reason. I would ask students to explain with specifics why they chose those particular pieces and to include a letter to the reader describing themselves as writers, identifying strengths, weaknesses, and goals. Less is more. Quality over quantity. Trust the process and the children.

Composing Third Portfolio Reincarnations: Learning to Be a Guide

As I began the third year of the Hudson Valley Project, I was truly beginning to understand how to invite my students to own their learning. We spent much of the first weeks of school sharing writing and discussing what made pieces successful and unsuccessful. We brainstormed qualities that successful pieces shared, and I discovered that I now had a much clearer picture of what these qualities were. I guided the discussion, and when important elements were missing I asked questions that elicited additions. The students were integrally involved in crafting the rubric that would guide their writing; they were internalizing what it was to be a good writer and we were working skillfully as a team. Once the rubric was completed, we practiced using it to evaluate pieces of writing. Then it became their tool to use to improve and evaluate their own writing.

In addition, together we created a list of questions that writers could ask themselves or peer writers that would help them to revise and improve their writing. These questions were grounded in the rubric and became the key to successful, student-crafted peer conferencing (Figure 5–11). The revisions improved twofold.

In the letters to the readers, the students' powerful responses, directed back at themselves and not at me, reflected their journeys as learners:

High-achieving learner: As a writer, I have gained many strengths. I use good language in many pieces. Instead of saying big, I say huge, humongous, colossal. I also have excellent use of commas. I use them in introductory phrases and to connect sentences . . . I have been using better and more interesting words. Before I used boring and dead language . . .

To overcome my weaknesses (finding ideas for stories, dialogue writing, not taking risks), I have set some goals for the next marking period. Goal number one is to take more risks. I will try new things in order to accomplish this. Goal number two is to use more dialogue. To accomplish this, I will try to put it in my stories, possibly even write full conversations.

I would like people to notice the language I use in my stories. I think long and hard about my language. I also really want people to notice my descriptions. I take pride in the way I describe things. I hope you, the reader, enjoy my stories.

Low-achieving learner: This is my writing portfolio. I worked very hard on these pieces. I hope you enjoy my pieces . . .

My strengths as writer is I am good at drafting, revising, conferencing, focus and organization and showing not telling. I love writing so I should be good at it. . . . Revising is the best part that I am good at. When I need to add more to a story I really fix it up. I put in interesting words and similes.

I have changed in writing by adding and fix up pieces of writing. In my stories I put some good words but not all the time. I have learned when you change a subject it's a different paragraph. When I write stories there are never bed to bed stories.

My weaknesses in writing are pre-writing and language. In pre-writing I never pre-write for some reason and I don't know why. I should pre-write

Figure 5–11
Conference Questions

Focus /Organization

- Does it flow?
- Does it make sense?
- Is it organized?
- Is there a clear purpose?
- Is there anything I don't need?
- Is this a bed-to-bed story?

Development

- Does the lead pull the reader in?
- Does it tie up loose parts?
- Does it sound like the end?
- Have I shown, not told, using examples?
- What's the most exiting part, and how can I build on it?
- Can my reader hear people talking? (quotes)

Language

- Did I use interesting words?
- Did I use good sentence structure? (not too short, or long and tangly)
- Did I use vivid language? (strong verbs)
- Did I use personal style? (voice)

Mechanics

- Did I punctuate and capitalize correctly?
- Did I spell correctly?
- Did I check my skill sheet?
- Did I use correct grammar?
- Did I use good sentences?

---

and I never do. In language, I don't use good words, but I should because it makes my story better and people like more interesting words.

My goals are projects. In projects that they assign I never turn them in on time. I don't turn them in on time because I always wait until the last minute to do them. I always forgot that I have a project to do. I think I should do them ahead of time and then I will have nothing to worry about.

In this letter, I want my reader to notice what things that I am having trouble with. Then I could go home and get help from my parents.

My previous portfolios never would have captured this level of thinking and reflection in different kinds of students, due in part to my insistence on directing my students' thinking. I have learned to be a guide, not a director; a facilitator, not a controller. I have learned to have faith in my students—to believe wholeheartedly that they have the capacity, if not eagerness, to take control of their own learning. It is my task to give them the tools and opportunities to do so.

6

The Crazy Project Lady Comes Home

Marcia Lubell
edited by Diana Muxworthy Feige

Over the years I had long given up that [traditional] model and had become known in my school as "that crazy project lady." More and more I tried to connect everything I taught to literature. I also was an early convert to writing process . . . I felt isolated in my efforts to reform my classroom and my teaching practices.

Marcia Lubell

Marcia Lubell is presently Teacher Coordinator of the English Department at Yorktown High School in Yorktown, New York. She has been teaching secondary English Language Arts for twenty-five years, primarily at the high school level. She is active as a consultant and staff developer in her district and others, as well as an instructor for the Northern Westchester Teacher Center, teaching courses in assessment and portfolio design. Marcia is coauthor of English for the Disenchanted *and* Language Works *and script writer for CD-ROMs on classic texts such as* Huckleberry Finn, Tom Sawyer, *and* The Scarlet Letter.

Marcia Lubell writes that the Hudson Valley Project reinforced her belief that assessment drives curriculum. Through the craftsmanship of designing portfolios, Marcia reinvented her classroom. More specifically, the articulation of focused, explicit outcomes changed Marcia's teaching practices; she realigned her curriculum and instruction in order to help her students achieve these newly stated

outcomes. Marcia then saw the power of her students' reflections—
their ongoing thinking about their strengths and weaknesses
as readers, writers, and thinkers. Marcia now believes that if
you give students the opportunity, structure, and guidance for
self-reflection they will revel in it, documenting their growth
and challenging themselves for future learning.

Sometime in the dark ages of the 1960s, I started teaching high school English. The model I followed was the one I had seen at college: I was the "expert" and asked all the questions; my students were vessels to be filled with the knowledge that only I could dispense. Though I experimented with trying to tie my course together with thematic ideas, basically I taught each strand separately—grammar on Monday, vocabulary on Tuesday, literature on Wednesday, writing on Thursday. Friday was test day. Throughout the week, the students sat rigidly in rows, and I did not allow talking except in response to my predetermined questions. We studied literature chronologically or by genres and were very concerned with textual analysis. It was almost as though I thought of my students as potential English majors.

A few decades later, in the 80s, I had long given up that model and had become known in my school as "that crazy project lady." More and more I tried to connect everything I taught to literature. I also was an early convert to process writing. I began experimenting with portfolios five years ago but except when I was working with one special colleague, Ruth Townsend, with whom I collaborated very closely, I felt isolated in my efforts to reform my classroom and my teaching practices. However, several years ago I was given the opportunity to join the Hudson Valley Portfolio Project, and that has made all the difference.

I was very cocky as I walked into that large room at Stony Point that first summer. After all, I had sample portfolios in my tote bag; my students already profited from the use of portfolios. I thought I had learned from experience all that I needed to know to make me an effective teacher. My first shock came as I listened to the presentation on outcomes. "What were our outcomes?" Giselle kept asking. We couldn't know what it was we wanted to accomplish with our portfolios unless we (1) predetermined exactly what it was we wanted our students to know and be able to do, and (2) designed our portfolios to reveal whether or not our students had accomplished these outcomes.

I was stunned. I had never really thought of that. We studied books, wrote essays about the books, developed projects designed to extend my students' creative ability to work with the ideas in those books. What more did I need?

Thinking in terms of outcomes was an epiphany for me; it changed my entire approach to designing my instruction and presented me with a whole new way of thinking, a new world of teaching. At the initial project meeting, we formed collaborative groups to formulate outcomes for our classrooms. My group came up with two major outcomes, one dealing with comprehension, the other with communication. They were:

1. Students should demonstrate their ability to react and interact with understanding with complex texts.

2. They should demonstrate their ability to communicate effectively, personally, analytically, and creatively.

Both of these outcomes seem very straightforward and hardly earth shattering. Indeed, many groups thought of similar outcomes. Yet the process of arriving at these outcomes proved critical in helping us to establish ownership of the project and to begin the thinking needed to develop a portfolio that would allow students to reveal their attainment of these general outcomes.

Together, we developed a series of indicators for these outcomes. For the comprehension outcome, the indicators included having students demonstrate that they read with depth of insight by collecting facts and ideas, discovering relationships, making inferences, making critical judgments, analyzing, evaluating, and drawing conclusions. For the communications outcome, we decided that students must express their ideas critically, organize their thoughts logically and coherently, and develop their ideas with appropriate and adequate support.

Again, none of this was utterly new. Intuitively, all of us had tried to move our students toward knowing and doing these things. However, spelling out the outcomes and indicators was especially significant for me. I went home from the first several days of that summer session eager to reexamine my units to ascertain the implications of this thinking about outcomes in my daily practices. What would it actually look like in my classroom to work from outcomes? I soon realized that I needed to make my indicators more concrete in order to design assignments that would truly lead to the attainment of each outcome. For comprehension, I determined that students needed to

Demonstrate that they could follow the twists and turns of the plot or development of idea in a text

Understand the motivations and personalities of the characters

Understand the effect of events and people on the characters

Appreciate stylistic elements and their effects

See connections to their own lives

For the communications outcome, I determined that students needed to

Demonstrate they could write convincingly

Develop a thesis and support it sufficiently

Use accurate and appropriate facts, details, examples, and direct references to support a thesis

Compare, analyze, synthesize, and apply new information

Pay attention to voice and audience

Use sophisticated style, word choice, phrasing, sentence structure, sentence variety, and coherence

Develop logical, appropriate organization with a beginning, middle, and end

Develop an engaging opening as well as an "as a result" conclusion

Armed with this myriad of specific attributes, I was able to design specific lessons to teach the skills necessary to elicit these attributes and, through them, the larger comprehension and communication outcomes.

Early in my consideration of what teaching strategies to adopt to fit my outcomes focus, I became concerned with how I would assess student outcomes. I decided to incorporate baseline and exit tasks in my portfolio design.[1] These would graphically reveal students' growth both in literary analysis and in communication. They would also allow students to experience and become aware of the tremendous progress they made toward comprehending complex textual materials and communicating that understanding in sophisticated and well-organized formal, creative, and personal written responses.

In practice, what was most rewarding to me as a teacher of heterogeneous students was that this outcome-based approach was successful both for my less able and for my high-achieving students. One student, who required the help of our resource room and was a mainstreamed special needs student, reflected on his progress:

> My "Story of an Hour" essay isn't even in essay form. It is very short and doesn't get to the point of the story. However, when I read "A Very Old Man With Enormous Wings," I understood the themes of the story. I used quotes to explain my understanding . . . I wrote it in essay form, and I got to the point. The last essay had run-ons; this one did not. My writing is totally different.
>
> It is like night and day. . . . Now that I am comparing my essays, I can't believe the difference . . . I think I have learned a lot this year. In the beginning

1. *Baseline tasks,* which I ask my students to complete before I give them any other instructions, help me find out what the students already know or are able to do. *Exit tasks* parallel baseline tasks, but are given to my students at the end of a unit or text to find out how much they've learned.

of the year I couldn't read a story and then write on it. Now I can do both. My
grammar was terrible at the beginning of the year. I think my grammar is 1000
times better, but I still need some work on it. (Joseph Savastano, June 1994)

Another student, accustomed to being academically successful, was equally
startled at her progress.

What boggles me is that I remember being somewhat pleased with my original baseline. It is only now that I can read over it and see the true mess that
it really is. For one thing, the whole thing lacked direction. My initial opening sentence did little more than state that I had read a story and a poem. Because of this crucial error, the rest of my essay was entirely irrelevant
because, in essence, I had never really proved anything . . . I merely ram-
bled. . . . Despite the fact that I think I could have done a better job on my final piece, I must admit that it was a vast improvement over my initial
attempts at this kind of writing. My final essay had direction; . . . my analysis of the two given works was much more advanced, both in organization
and in presentation of argument. . . . I cannot get over how tremendous these
differences are. I am thankful to be able to see true evidence of how effective this year's English course really was. (Sonia Werner, June 1995)

The focus on achievement of outcomes with very clear skill-based performance indicators led to a more accurate student self-reflection on growth
and performance and changed my daily classroom practice in dramatic ways.
Philosophically, the shift moved from the study of texts for their own sake toward developing the skills students needed to interpret with confidence *any*
demanding text. By framing the course with baseline and exit tasks, I clarified
for my students and for myself exactly what work my students needed to do
during the year.

In addition, articulating the specifics of what the attainment of each outcome would look like in terms of performance indicators led me to reexamine
each of my instructional units. I began to focus the units on tasks that would
provide opportunities for students to develop comprehension and communication skills needed for the exit tasks. Thus, from the very beginning of my
work with the Hudson Valley Project, I quickly realized that my task was not
merely the design of a portfolio as an assessment tool but also the design of
an entire outcome-based curriculum, with my assessment embedded within
my daily classroom instructional practices. The cocky project lady was not so
cocky anymore. I had quite a learning journey ahead of me, yet I also knew
that I had already undergone a fundamental transformation.

A *Macbeth* Unit Serves as a Prelude to Portfolio Design

After the end of that first summer session, I worked on what was loosely
known as my portfolio design. However, what I actually worked on was my
classroom and unit design. I went back to each junior year unit and reworked

it around the idea of outcomes and indicators, letting the outcomes of the unit shape particular assignments. Each assignment would in turn ground and shape all the instruction for that particular text.

One example of such a unit was the study of Shakespeare's *Macbeth*. My initial outcomes were the same for this text as for others: I wanted my students to be able to react to and interact with the text with understanding, and I wanted them effectively to communicate personally, analytically, and creatively about their understanding of the text. At the same time, I was interested in having them accomplish some outcomes specific to the issues raised by this play. I wanted them to understand and appreciate the effect of unlimited power on individuals—to internalize the corrosive effects of ambition, of the lust for violence, and of believing that the ends justifies the means. Most important, I was interested in guiding them to see the need to take responsibility for their actions and to understand the consequences that result from certain kinds of actions. Outcomes provided shape and unity to my approach to teaching texts. In a similar way, an authentic context provided my students with multiple opportunities to hone the skills they needed to attain the outcomes.

The context I established for the study of *Macbeth* was the collaborative creation of newspapers. In the past, as the "project lady," I might also have had students create a *Macbeth* newspaper, but the project would have occurred after the formal study of the play as an "add-on"—something separate from the serious study of the work: the analysis. Now the newspaper became the lens through which we studied the Macbeths and their abuse of power as well as their rise and fall from power. For example, when students completed act 2 of *Macbeth,* in which Macbeth murders the king and assumes the throne, students showed they understood the intricacies of the characters and events as they wrote news articles, in small groups, about Duncan's death, editorials eulogizing the kindly king's rule, and opinion pieces speculating on the causes of the murder and the identity of the murderer(s). After each act, groups returned to their newspapers and worked on relevant articles specific to the events that had unfolded. By the end of the study of the play, groups had a repertoire of newspaper articles from which to construct their final project piece, the *Macbeth* newspaper.

By focusing immediately on the unit project and by designing the project so that it reinforced the outcomes and indicators, I clarified the direction and purpose of the study without sacrificing anything of importance in the process. My assessment of student outcomes became thoroughly embedded within the fabric of my daily instruction instead of being an isolated event that occurred at the end of each unit. Students knew where they were going and how to get there. And so did I. Outcome-based classroom planning organized my teaching in ways that made sense to me and worked well for my students.

Yet without the impetus of the Hudson Valley Project, the continued en-

couragement of participants, and feedback from group sessions and conferences with Giselle, I never would have redesigned my classroom in this way.
One of the most helpful components of the project was that we were not abandoned to our own efforts after that one week in the summer. We met monthly,
either in caucus groups or as a whole, and we received regular feedback about
the development of our designs. We practiced what we were implementing in
our classrooms. We reflected on what we were doing and on our responses to
those changes. In one of these reflections, I summarized my own learning:

> As far as teaching practices are concerned, the major difference I see is that
> I am working backwards from clearly stated outcomes and have formulated
> in writing for myself and for my students exactly how we will master these
> outcomes. These units, articulated in my portfolio, are a major departure for
> me. While I have done many, if not most, of the same lessons before, I had
> never before clarified for myself what it was that I expected to accomplish
> with each of the tasks I set for students. It was useful for me as well as reas-
> suring. Instead of believing as I had for many years that all I was doing was
> "teaching books," one title after another, I saw the intuitive logic that had
> been there all along and felt pretty good about what I was doing and more
> sure of why.

Appreciating the Power of Student Reflection

The first year of the project was over. I was very pleased with the results of
my students' portfolios and the seriousness with which they had taken this ar-
duous task. I saw graphically displayed just how much growth my students
had experienced in the areas of comprehension and communication. More important, *they* could see their growth in black and white and, often for the first
time, realize that they could be successful communicators and that they had
developed dramatically in their competence in English. One particularly gratifying example came from a student who had previously been tracked in a
nonregents class and felt inadequate when she first transferred into my Regents class.[2] In her self-analysis, she alludes to the progress she made in creative and personal writing as well as in more analytical writing:

> I am pleased with my transition from English CR to English R. It is even
> more satisfying to know that my work has been critiqued by a Regents de-
> termined criteria. That I was, for the most part, successful, is a testimony to
> my overall growth as a reader, writer, and thinker . . . I'd like to say that
> generally, as a reader I have experienced a wide variety of literature—from
> stories like "The Story of an Hour" to novels such as "A Scarlet Letter." I've
> read old manuscripts—Macbeth—to modern plays—"The Death of a Sales-
> man." Each one has been a challenge in its own way. I have developed the

---

2. *Regents* are the New York State–mandated exit tests for a Regents diploma.

use and expression of writing personas. I can see, feel, act, and react as if I am the character. This is evident in my readers' logs and my successful writing of an original ending to *Catcher In the Rye* and Zeena's letter based on *Ethan Frome*. I have made great strides in the area of creative writing. I have learned to organize my thoughts and follow through with description and dialogue. This is seen in my parody "An Adventure of Hank Finn." I really enjoyed developing Hank's character and having him speak my thoughts. . . . As a thinker I have demonstrated increased appreciation of literature. I have shown this in my essay on the Abuse of Power and "My Editorial on Women" which was motivated by my reading and reflection on Lady Macbeth. In the former, I used the concept of abuse and substantiated it with specifics from Macbeth, and Night, comparing them with modern-day illustrations. (Adrienne Oshman, June 1994)

Adrienne's reflection on her own achievements reveals again how an outcome-based approach gives students multiple opportunities and needed skills to succeed. In fact, reflections such as Adrienne's were so compelling that they forced me to rethink my outcomes. In the second year of the project, I added a reflection outcome: Students will demonstrate that they can reflect with accuracy and understanding on their strengths and weaknesses as readers, writers, and thinkers.

From the beginning of my work with portfolios, I had always included student reflections, but I had not recognized the importance of training students to reflect with greater skill. Once I realized just how important reflection was to students' academic proficiency, I incorporated reflection into every aspect of their performances. Students reflected each time they wrote for me. I spent considerable time and energy in guiding students to create more precise analyses of their own products, and then to use those personal judgments to inform their own work so that they could improve and master the outcomes. They described their thought processes, their work habits, their satisfaction with certain aspects of each piece they created, their concerns and problems, and the new learning that resulted. With each succeeding attempt at reflection, students became more adept, more self-analytical, and more empowered. Again, baseline and exit samples were very revealing. Anthony Cacciola, an eleventh grader, wrote the following as his first reflection of the year:

Reading: I love reading but I have trouble with big projects.

Writing: I'm not very good at writing, and I usually can't handle long-terms projects. I have little imagination.

Thinking: I'm a slow thinker for things I don't understand. I'm fast at things I do understand. I need time to figure out things to write, like certain projects you need to make up a situation or a scenario; I can't usually do it at a normal speed because I have to think for a while.

A short excerpt from his final reflection reveals just how far he had come, both in self-esteem and in reflecting on his work:

> I am very proud of myself . . . I have learned so many things about myself from doing this portfolio. I have learned that I was a horrible writer at the beginning of the year, but I have managed to bring my skill in writing up at this point. I think it took a good review of myself, in how I think about things and how I follow through with them to realize that I was able to do so much better than what I was doing. I think that I have definitely grown in one aspect; I now take my time and go over everything before I start to write or do something.

By the time students write reflections for their portfolios, they are able to comment very concretely and astutely on the degree to which their outcome-based work, culminating in the final portfolio, has changed their perceptions of themselves. The process works equally well for students of all ability levels. Just as we see the growth in Anthony's reflections, it is also clear in the work of a student accustomed to academic success. She writes,

> It is funny how growth kind of sneaks up on you. I honestly didn't realize how much I had changed as a reader, writer, and thinker until I was able to do this project. . . . I feel that my greatest and most substantial growth occurred in my essay writing. Here is where I learned to write more concretely, to focus, and to eliminate much of the unnecessary verbiage that would often infect my writing. . . . I think that one of the most important things about this year was the kinds of work that we did. I was able to experiment with English in ways that I never had before. Whether it was writing a handbook for the proper way to handle Native American culture (a final project for *When the Legends Die* by Hal Borland) or creating a video retrospective for *Huckleberry Finn* by Mark Twain, I found myself exploring English while using a variety of new and more innovative techniques. . . . Yet, despite all these things, I know that I still have quite a lot to work on. . . . I do have a tendency to 'go all over the place' and sometimes I fear that this habit of getting a little overwhelmed affects my work. . . . I have to work on pacing myself for many times I will spend literally hours on things that could have been done in a period. . . . This year has been an enormous challenge. It is really only now (it being almost June) that I am able to look back and see all that I have gained. . . . (Sonia Werner, June 1995)

Resolving Dissonance

The more involved I became with using portfolios to assess my students, the more I sensed a mismatch between what I needed to do to find out what my students knew and were able to do and the traditional English Regents exam. With my portfolio, students had multiple opportunities, crafted over time, to demonstrate their attainment of the comprehension, communication, and reflection outcomes. They could revise and learn from earlier mistakes; they could take the time necessary to perfect their work, to create finished pieces, to show what they really *could* do. With the traditional exam, particularly the 45 points of multiple-choice questions and the time-constrained essay questions, students were primarily revealing what they could *not* do—what they did *not* know.

The emphasis was all wrong. I decided to apply for a 35 percent variance in which I would seek to replace the multiple-choice sections of the regents examination (vocabulary, spelling, and reading comprehension), with the portfolio. To do that I modified my intended outcomes and my portfolio design. First, I blended my comprehension and communication outcomes with the New York State English Language Arts Standards—in which students were to demonstrate that they could read, write, speak and listen for information and understanding, for literary response and expression, for critical analysis, and for social interaction.

This required a number of changes in the portfolio menu, but I was willing to find the time and harness the energy to identify them because I could no longer live with the dissonance. I wanted to see if I could resolve the injustice imposed on my students. To accommodate the "information and understanding" standard, I invited students to include a piece from another subject. Many chose research papers in history, science reports, and so on. The "literary response and expression and critical analysis" standards were already richly represented by the students' creative and analytical written course work. In order to accommodate the "social interaction" standard, I required students to present their portfolios to groups of interested peers and adults.

I also was concerned that if I replaced the reading comprehension and vocabulary sections of the traditional Regents exam, I would miss the opportunity to assess those skills. This is where the baseline and exit tasks came in.

I was on a roll with these changes, increasingly convinced of their merits. Over time, I continued to change the portfolio to place more emphasis on the students' attainment of the articulated outcomes. I asked students to include a letter to the reader in which they articulated what they found meaningful in each book and their strengths and weaknesses as readers. They included reflections on their development as writers, readers, and thinkers, and I created specific rubrics for each portfolio category. I wanted the portfolio to be as full a mirror as possible of what students knew and could do. I wanted students to look at their portfolios and see themselves, past, present, and future.

Authentic Assessment and Its Response to the Challenge of Heterogeneity

Perhaps the most important change in the second year of the portfolio project resulted from the newly heterogeneous nature of the classes that were developing portfolios, composed of Regents and non-Regents students. Just as the outcome-based approach to my assessment and curriculum planning caused me to revamp my approach to teaching, the prospect of greater student diversity sent me back to the drawing board. I had certain bottom-line assumptions; I was determined that my classes were not going to be any less challenging for the brightest of my students than they had been before. However, I had to find meaningful ways to tap into the strengths of those who had not traditionally been a part of my Regents classes. By using more authentic, real-world group tasks, I hoped to address the needs of students at all ends of the academic spectrum.

To begin, I decided to modify assignments I had used in the past. First, I asked students to take a theme from *Macbeth;* develop it into a child-oriented moral tale about loyalty, the sharing of power, the limits of ambition, and so on; and work in pairs to create a book for an elementary school class. This project was truly an authentic task: it involved a real audience, a real product, an exhibition component, and a real-world deadline. Students found they had to consider their audience in determining how to write their story—how involved it should be, how much dialogue it should have, how to make it visually appealing, and how to read it in an interesting way to young children. They also had to pay closer attention to mechanics than usual to avoid the embarrassment of making a mistake in grammar or spelling in a book to be read by children. In preparation, they reviewed their own favorite children's books, analyzed the books' components, talked to a published children's book author, and considered very seriously their task of working with small children. They prepared questions to initiate discussion and worked hard at crafting their stories so they would be entertaining, visually attractive, and instructive.

As a result of this unit's reshaping and its encouraging success, I created other authentic group projects for a number of my literature units. For example, in the past, I had asked students to create a letter from the character Tom Black Bull to his school detailing the harm their educational methods had exerted on him (*When the Legends Die* by Hal Borland). Now I asked student groups to craft training manuals for new teachers of Native American students. Instead of asking students to write an essay on censorship for *Catcher in the Rye,* I asked them to create a booklet from the psychiatrists at Lubell Cozy Acres Rest Home to the Governing Board that discussed whether Holden Caulfield was ready to be released from treatment and sent home. When we read *Huckleberry Finn,* students prepared a video retrospective of scenes from the book that developed a particular theme and taped a panel discussion debating a controversial issue surrounding that theme. In the past, I would have asked them simply to write an analytical essay.

While both my traditional assignments and the new project assignments provided opportunities for students to demonstrate the comprehension and communication outcomes, the second set of assignments was more authentic, richer, multilayered, and engaging. Moreover, many of the new assignments required group work and therefore addressed the New York State Standard for social interaction in ways my individual essay assignments had not. As a result of assignments like these, students of different ability levels could participate successfully in far more demanding assessments of their comprehension and communication than I had ever witnessed before. They were making meaning from complex texts and communicating effectively with their audiences in personal, analytical, and/or creative ways. They were growing before my very eyes.

Yorktown High School Buzzes

After I applied to the state for the 35 percent variance, all of the eleventh-grade English teachers at Yorktown High School became involved in the project. For the first time in our school's history, the entire eleventh grade took the Regents exam, and more than 230 students used their portfolios as 35 points of their total score. In tabulating our results, we were pleased to find that students' scores on the portfolio section were very comparable to their performance on the more standardized portion of the exam; indeed, grades for the portfolios tended to be slightly lower, indicating the greater rigor of our portfolio assessments as compared to the state-designed portion of the exam. Moreover, we had a 90 percent passing rate overall.

Throughout the school, students worked together in heterogeneous classes, were challenged by the demands of the portfolio to perform at their optimum levels, and for the most part succeeded in meeting that challenge. It was exciting to watch the change in students' attitudes as the due date for the portfolios approached. Students who had never taken English as seriously as subjects such as science or math suddenly began focusing enormous energy on outdoing everyone else to make the content and appearance of their portfolios the very best they could. Droves of students sought extra help as they began sifting through the year's work to uncover promising pieces to rework for the portfolio. When conscientious students brought in completed portfolios with pages encased in plastic, students who had not done so took note and worked harder to keep up. As they considered the required exit task, they asked questions such as "I need another joining word to get me from one idea to the next. I'm bored with *also*. What other joining words could I use?"

> I think the poem is about child abuse, but the word 'romped' means played around according to the dictionary. Why can't I fit that meaning into my interpretation?

The entire school buzzed with talk of the portfolios. It was almost as though English had finally come of age. And I, the "crazy project lady," had finally come home. Suzanne Verneau, an eleventh-grade English teacher, noted:

> I can't believe how much learning is going on here. My students look at what they wrote at the beginning of the year and they can't believe that was their work. They have come SO far, and the portfolio is helping them realize exactly how far and in what specific ways.

Looking Backward and Forward

Because of the very encouraging results of the 1995 portfolios and the suc-cess of our students in the Regents exam, the English teachers and I decided to apply for a 100 percent variance for 1996. We knew without doubt that the amount of work students put into the portfolios represented far more than the 35 points allotted to the 1995 variance. The Department of Education re-sponded favorably. We are now one of a select number of high schools in New York who are exempt from New York State Regents exams.

The saga, though, does not end here. Revisions have become a way of life. While still struggling to help my students achieve comprehension, com-munication, and reflection outcomes, I added an additional outcome for the upcoming school years. My students must demonstrate their increasing ability to work independently. I am also designing more and more instructional strategies that require my students to take a greater responsibility for their own learning.

Clearly, my experience with the Hudson Valley Project has reinforced my belief that assessment drives curriculum. Portfolio assessment has provided me with a more sophisticated, authentic way of viewing student performance. Moreover, I have discovered that portfolio development and its basis in agreed-upon outcome compels me to develop an outcome-driven curriculum that reflects the same authenticity and focus as the portfolios. I have changed my daily classroom practices, the focus of my instruction, the projects I as-sign, and the nature of my demands for student performance. I have rein-vented my classroom in order to help my students learn and achieve. The intricate instructional units now give students multiple opportunities to demonstrate their competence in each of the outcomes.

Slowly but surely I am finding ways to show what students know and can do. I am finding ways to mirror who they are and who they can be. The jour-ney has been exciting and valuable. I look forward to continuing to evolve as I devise more authentic ways for my students to become competent in essen-tial language arts' skills. My students in many ways have been my teachers. I thank them and wish them well in their life journeys.

7

Ongoing Assessment Strategies Allow Me to Meet the Needs of My Students

Liz Locatelli
edited by Diane Cunningham

In looking more closely at my students through their projects, reflections, and portfolios, I learned a great deal about their needs and my own shortcomings as a teacher.

Liz Locatelli

Liz Locatelli is an English teacher at North Rockland High School, where she has taught for twenty-five years. She is also an adjunct professor for the reading and special education department of Long Island University. Liz is currently mentoring master's degree candidates at the City College of New York by guiding them through the design and writing of their theses. Liz's current assessment priority is the refinement of a summer program for ninth graders, called Jumpstart, which was created to find out how teachers at North Rockland High School can best meet the needs of this student population. As part of Jumpstart, an interdisciplinary team of teachers is using portfolio assessment to inform their instruction and assessment practices during the year.

This chapter exemplifies the assumption that good assessment cannot exist independently of good instruciton. Liz Locatelli's experiences adjusting her assessment practices highlight the point that assessment can only be understood or developed in conjunction with supporting

*curriculum and instruction. This chapter clearly shows that
assessment is intrinsically tied to what teachers value, to
what they teach, and to how they teach.*

Five years ago I was happily congratulating myself on my ability to "set kids up for success." I had developed such explicit plans and could articulate my expectations so clearly that I was convinced that any student could succeed in my class, provided he or she did exactly what I required each step of the way. It isn't surprising that I felt upset with any student who did not succeed. I had told the students what was significant in each book we read and how to organize their essays. What more did they want? I generally blamed student failures on lack of motivation.

In 1993 I joined the Hudson Valley Portfolio Assessment Project and began experimenting with assessment strategies, trying to find ways to determine more accurately what students did and did not understand. I wanted to find out what was blocking their understanding so that I could provide instruction and support that would enable them to succeed. I began to give my students more opportunities to articulate orally or in writing what they had learned. I became a researcher in my own classroom, experimenting with various assessment strategies and looking closely at what students were saying and writing. The experience proved humbling as well as rewarding. In looking more closely at my students through their projects, reflections, and portfolios, I learned a great deal about their needs and my own shortcomings as a teacher.

During my involvement in the project I used various forms of assessments—some authentic, some less authentic, but all valuable. I revised my traditional methods of assessing my students in ways that would allow me to see more of what they were thinking, what they understood, and what they were struggling with. My assessments became more open ended and, as a result, more effective in helping me guide my students in developing the knowledge, skills, and attitudes they need to succeed, both in my classroom and throughout their lives.

Revising My Traditional Assessments

Vocabulary Quizzes

When I began experimenting with assessment strategies, I looked for an alternative to the multiple-choice quizzes I had given in the past. I began by looking at my vocabulary quizzes. I asked myself, What do I want the students to know or be able to do as a result of our work with vocabulary? I wanted the students to be able to understand the words when they see them in texts and to use them effectively in their oral and written communications. With these outcomes in mind, I asked students to give me the definition or a synonym of each word and then to use each word in a sentence. I hoped that this assessment would tell me who had studied and who truly understood the meaning of the word.

A close look at my students' responses showed me much more than I had expected. Students who knew "out of date" was the definition of *obsolete* wrote sentences such as, "We couldn't drink the milk because it was obsolete." Students who had memorized *innocent* as a synonym for *ingenuous* wrote sentences such as, "I told the judge I was ingenuous because I didn't do it." These inaccurate responses made me realize it was possible that students who had failed miserably on multiple-choice tests *had* studied, perhaps had memorized a synonym that did not help them to make the correct choice on the test because the synonym was too narrow or because it had led them to some erroneous interpretation of the word's meaning.

I decided to investigate the validity of my multiple-choice tests further by asking students to write definitions and sentences and then answer multiple-choice questions for the same words. A look at the results from four students showed me the test's limitations of my multiple-choice tests. Jeanna and Megan both scored 80 percent on the multiple-choice quiz. However, Megan could actually define all of the words and use them appropriately, while Jeanna could only use two of the words correctly, indicating that she had simply memorized a synonym and had not understood the meaning or use of the word. Although Treina received a 60 percent on the multiple-choice quiz, a look at her definitions and sentences indicated that she could only demonstrate an understanding of two of the words and that she must have made some lucky guesses on the multiple-choice test. Brigida, who scored lower than Treina on the multiple-choice quiz (50 percent), was actually able to define 80 percent of the words. She was also able to use three of them correctly in sentences.

Clearly, my revised vocabulary assessment provided a more accurate picture of what my students understood and could do. As I began to see assessment as ongoing and formative rather than as evaluative and summative, I gave students a chance to try out their sentences before the test. We had regular practice sessions in which I helped students to work through their misconceptions and to understand why their interpretation of a word might be too narrow or might not help them to truly understand its meaning. As assessment became a learning tool in my classroom, the atmosphere in the class changed. Students realized that it was OK to make mistakes and in fact better to make an error and learn how to correct it than to cover up what they did not understand. Students became less threatened and more accountable for their learning. Those who had studied and then struggled to make the distinctions required on multiple-choice tests came to feel that their efforts were acknowledged. Students who were skilled at taking conventional tests realized that they needed to put forth more effort in their studies.

At the same time, I came to understand that there *is* some value in continuing to give multiple-choice quizzes in vocabulary. My honors students showed me that sometimes the multiple-choice tests pose a greater challenge than writing definitions and sentences because students have to consider nuances and use flexible thinking to figure out which answer is best. In light of the importance placed on the Regents and SAT exams, I have decided to periodically give multiple-choice tests. No single method of assessment can meet all of my needs; I must consider what I want for each group of students and match the assessment to that objective.

Reading Checks

My new insights caused me to look at other assessments I was using. Like many of my colleagues, I had in the past often used a short-answer or multiple-choice quiz that was easy to grade to check that the students had done their outside reading. On many occasions, the students' poor performance on these quizzes had led me to think that they had not done all of the reading, even though some of them swore that they had. Some students had also told me that they saw no point in reading at home since they didn't pass the quizzes either way. "Why bother?" they asked.

I began to approach students who had failed, asking them to tell me what they knew about the text. I was amazed at what I heard. In many cases they knew a lot, but not in the areas covered by the quiz. In other cases, I found that misinterpretations or the inability to see the connections between sentences or the relationships between ideas had caused them to draw conclusions that seemed absurd to me. Several students could give me facts but had no idea of the meaning of the text as a whole. Finally, I found that prior knowledge or preconceived attitudes about a subject had led some students to draw erroneous conclusions.

In response, I revised my reading checks so that they are more open ended. They allow students to discuss what they know and to react to what they have read. I now do reading checks, not only to determine who is keeping up with the reading but also to find out how accurately the students are comprehending and interpreting what they are reading. These checks are also designed to help students focus on the sections they will later need for projects. They have become learning tools as well as assessment tools.

For example, as the students read *The Adventures of Huckleberry Finn,* they knew that I would eventually ask them to form an opinion about Twain's treatment of African Americans. Their final task would be to prepare a speech for a mock schoolboard meeting at which we would debate whether or not the book was appropriate for high school students in our district at this time. They knew they would have to support their opinions with evidence from the book. Therefore, at the end of the first section, as part of my first reading check, I asked the students to react to Huck and to Jim. I asked them to write down words that they felt described each character, to provide specific references to support these generalizations, and to explain how they felt about each character. At that point I wanted them to see that Huck and Tom were adventurous, mischievous boys who played pranks on Jim and enjoyed watching his gullible reaction to their antics. In a later section, after Huck plays a prank on Jim, I asked the students to discuss how the incident shows a change in Huck's attitude toward Jim.

For reading checks like these, I allow the students to use their books, but only give them fifteen minutes to complete the assignment. Students who have not read at home are not able to find what they need because they don't know what to look for. Those who have a general sense of the text have the added security of being able to check their facts. And the students who have read the text are encouraged to reread for specific evidence. This rereading reinforces their knowledge of the text, develops the habit of reading closely for a particular purpose, and enables them to support answers with specific references. These checks have helped students assess their own understanding as well. They are able to ask questions and I am able to provide the individual support to help each student understand the text.

I have come to call these assessments "qualifiers." Before students can write an essay, participate in a discussion, or take a test on the content, they have to perform satisfactorily on the qualifier. This holds each student accountable and gives me an opportunity to clarify what each student has not understood as well as to find out who is not prepared. The students find this nonthreatening and fair. They have come to believe that I'm working with them and not trying to trap them. In fact, it is not uncommon for students to approach me before class to ask for an extension because they need to read more before they take the qualifier.

The qualifiers do not take long to check. I am able to determine who is ready for the next step and who needs more time or assistance. Sometimes I find that the class as a whole needs assistance, so I stop and provide the support or direct instruction that I feel is needed. Not every student now reads everything assigned, but my reading checks have become valuable learning tools for my students and for me.

Regents Tests

As I continued to question the validity of multiple-choice tests as a sole assessment, I knew I needed more proof. So, I conducted another experiment with the poem "Mending Wall," by Robert Frost. I asked my students, who were seeing the poem for the first time, to write a paragraph explaining what they thought Frost was trying to say. Then I gave them a Regents-type multiple-choice test that included two questions that tested their ability to use syntax cues, two questions that required them to recognize poetic techniques, five questions that required them to make inferences, and one question that required them to recognize the main idea. The following are the narrative responses of three average students who were preparing to take the English Regents in eleventh grade:

> Frost is telling me in this poem that people that could get along have walls between them for no reason they put them up because someone told them to. Some have a lack of understanding. They don't know why they put up the wall the something that doesn't love the wall is the feeling of that neighbor who put the wall and the other neighbor.

> In the "Mending Wall", the wall comes down in the winter time. In the spring time they build it back up again. The narrator doesn't think the wall is necessary but the neighbor has to build it up again because he doesn't want to go against his father's word. I think walls are necessary when you need to get away from people, but I don't think they are necessary when you are pressured into building a wall.

> The poem the *Mending Wall* by Robert Frost explains what happens to people during the seasons of the year and how hunters come and break the wall between Frost and his neighbor and every spring they both go to the wall And mend it so that there are no gaps between them. He also talks about how they really don't need the wall because they are good friends. Frost thinks that the hunters or his neighbor could be taking the rocks off of the wall. The poem means that some boundaries that separate people are artificial and unnecessary.

The student who wrote the first response scored 90 percent on the multiple-choice test. Despite the fact that he was not able to make sense of the poem, he was able to look closely at the text and to find bits and pieces of information that answered the questions. His success on the quiz was due mainly to the fact that he was to match specific text references to the correct answer. His summary, unfortunately, indicates that while he was able to deal with the meaning of specific lines, he was not able to make sense of the poem as a whole.

The second student, on the other hand, scored only 70 percent on the quiz, despite the fact that he had a good grasp of the meaning of the poem. His summary also indicates that he thought about the poem and reacted to it at a personal level. His own feeling about walls and his apparent desire for privacy at times seemed to help him to develop more fully his understanding of the author's message.

The third student earned only 30 percent on the multiple-choice test. His summary, however, indicates that his incorrect answers were probably the result of miscues rather than of lack of involvement. First, he focused on the introduction and expected the poem to be about why the wall requires mending. Then he picked up on the line "The work of hunters is another thing," and concluded that hunters were important to the poem. Since he could picture hunters messing up the wall, he missed the fact that Frost dismisses this as the reason why the wall needs repair.

This analysis of my test and the student work solidified my conclusion that multiple-choice tests alone are not valid indicators of students' ability to comprehend text.

Incorporating Authentic Assessment

The success of my ongoing assessment practices caused me to reconsider the way I was evaluating my students' content knowledge. I became dissatisfied with the short-answer questions that I was using to evaluate their knowledge of the literature and of the period. I began to think that my students could and would do more if I gave them projects that afforded them more flexibility, more choice, and more time. As a result, I found myself ready to listen when Giselle Martin-Kniep suggested using authentic assessment tasks. My first attempt was a project for the Puritan unit. In considering what was essential in this unit, I determined that I really wanted the students to understand the relationship between the philosophy of a people, their writings, and their lifestyle. I then decided that there were several ways in which students could demonstrate what they knew about the period and the writings of that period and show how the thinking of the times affected the lives of the Puritans. For example, a student could keep a diary as a Puritan, write a letter to family in England, present a conversation between a Puritan and a Native American, and so on. The format did not matter as long as the project showed an understanding of the attitudes and beliefs of the Puritans and reflected the manners and lifestyle of the times.

The first year that I attempted this long-term project, I maintained strict control over the content by telling the students which works to read prior to the writing. The second year, impressed with the interest and enthusiasm shown by the students in the first year, I also required that students would do their own research in the library. I was truly amazed at the variety of sources they found and at the fascinating information they uncovered. Many of the students reported that the information they had found on their own was much more interesting than what they had learned in class. The creative aspect of the projects also allowed them to demonstrate their understanding of the times as well as a knowledge of the facts. One student began her project by describing her reaction to Reverend Edward's sermon:

> "A wrathful God holds you over the pit of hell as much as one holds a spider
> of some loathsome insect over the fire." I sat entrapped in the high pews of
> our simple meeting house enthralled by Reverend Jonathan Edwards' views

of a condemning, spiteful God. I thought of how worthless and loathsome I must appear in the eyes of God and the anger He feels when looking at my sins. He must view me with the same abhorrence and detest that I have when I look at a spider. My daughter clung to the linen of my Sabbath frock coat as I felt her innocent body shaking with repressed fear at the minister's harsh, violent words.

While not all students were able to blend knowledge, creativity, and a facility with language to create such wonderful pieces, the majority of my students created projects that were interesting and informative. The following excerpt is taken from the work of a Regents student:

The Indians took my brother and I to a small village for a feast at which Jason and I broke into a commentary about our Puritan life and beliefs:
"Our beliefs are actually kind of simple," I said.
"True Brian, true. We have a holy book called the Bible. Our study is centered around hearing the word from the pulpit of the church," Jason continued. "What we do is read passages, analyze them and use these parts to enable us to live day by day. The church reviews various passages and helps us to understand them. Our beliefs are such a part of us that our schools and our government are also determined by our religious beliefs."
I then explained, "Education is one of the most important parts of our civilization. In order for us to be able to read the Word we must be able to read. We cannot and do not want to be illiterate. It is because education is so important to the Puritan people that Massachusetts enacted the first provision for free public schools in this country. Any town of fifty families or more must get the money to pay a teacher."

The students who were not able to handle the creative aspects produced factual reports:

This report is from the Puritans to the Indians on reasons why the Indians should let us Puritans stay in your area and become friends with you the Indians.
In our beliefs religion is a top priority. God is a part of our lives. We think that if we are very good we can be one of the chosen ones and be given immortality. We should not do anything wrong because god can do terrible things. So if we were afraid of god we obviously won't do anything to make god do something terrible to us.

There are clearly various levels of performance for various aspects of the project. I chose to evaluate the students' depth, specificity and accuracy of content, ability to relate to content and to leave a memorable impression, and ability to use standard English correctly. I gave the students a rubric that described levels of performance in each of those aspects. They knew ahead of time how I would grade them, and through conferences they translated the rubric into their own words and used it to assess their work along the way. Each aspect was marked separately on the rubric so that, for example, students who achieved only a low level on creativity could still be recognized as achieving a high level for the specificity and development of their content.

The students' response was very positive. Not only did they learn more, but they also developed a much better understanding of what they had read, and they referred to this knowledge many times throughout the year. Furthermore, their attitude about the Puritan period changed drastically. In a reflection essay, one honors student reported:

> At first I was frustrated with the topic and the task. I had little interest in the topic. When it was explained that I could choose my own direction, I was able to overcome my frustrations and apply creativity to my research.
>
> I began my research on the Puritans in a general direction. As my research progressed, I became fascinated by the foundations of Puritanism and its influence not only on the Puritan society of the 1600's but on today's society. I was able to see the connection between some of the values and morals of traditional American culture and their roots in Pre-Colonial New England. I became more involved in research and I not only learned the material but understood it.

Encouraged by the success of this project, I decided to try another. This project required the students to imagine that they had visited with Thoreau, Emerson, or Bryant to discuss the author's life and work. They could present what they had learned as a result of this imaginary encounter in a variety of ways. I had always struggled to get students through the readings of the transcendentalists. However, these philosophers came alive for the class when a colleague of mine volunteered to pose as Henry David Thoreau so that the students could ask him some questions in preparation for their next project.

Again, this was a long-term project, and everything we did during the course of the unit was directly related to the students' final tasks. Prior to the interview with my colleague, the students had to research Thoreau's life and works so that they could ask meaningful questions. The interview helped many students get a sense of how to shape their projects. It also gave them all an opportunity to clarify ideas they found confusing and to relate more personally to the author.

Some students wrote out interviews. Others wrote letters or diaries reflecting on their experiences. The form did not matter as long as they reacted in some way to the man's philosophy. The students became very involved in the project and most of them developed a real appreciation of the philosopher. One student wrote a short story that cast Thoreau in a new role as her guardian angel who appeared to comfort her and give her advice. In her reflection, she wrote:

When I wrote my Thoreau story, I tried to put Thoreau into a body and personality that teenagers could accept. I think Henry Thoreau's image can be a little intimidating. I mean, who wants to read about some old, bearded guy who lived in the woods for two years. You have to really understand his beliefs well before you can respect them and relate them to modern society. It's only then that you can admire his tremendous contribution to society. I wrote my story hoping to make Thoreau's work a little easier to understand and fun to read.

As I'm writing this reflection essay, I'm reading the story I wrote. I see a lot of myself in my main character, Julia. I patterned Thoreau after a guardian angel and I effectively presented Thoreau's work so that it wouldn't seem so complicated. I sort of hid Thoreau's message in my story.

It was interesting to see how students incorporated the content into their projects. One student tried to clarify for her readers a point about Emerson that she felt might be misunderstood. In her description of her imaginary interview, she asked Emerson, "In your essay 'Self-Reliance' your main point was to trust yourself. In your life did you have experiences that caused you to believe you could not rely on others, or did you just believe that you had to live by your own conscience?" She then gave Emerson's reply:

When I was eight years old my father died so I had to grow up without a father for a role model. Two of my brothers died of tuberculosis and mental problems and another brother spent his life in a mental institution. I had to learn to rely on myself. Then my first wife, Ellen, died after only two years of marriage. My first son, Waldo, died in 1842. I was lonely in that respect, but I did have friends from the Transcendental Club which published the magazine, *The Dial*. However, that is not what I was talking about. I believe that people should form their own opinions first, before listening to anyone else. And they should trust their own opinions and go with them. In my essay "Self-Reliance" I wrote, "What I must do is all that concerns me." I have to be true to my own conscience and not worry about what others might say about me.

I was also amazed at the level of personal involvement that these projects prompted. One student, an amateur writer of prose and poetry, chose to meet the task requirements by writing an imaginary interview between herself and William Cullen Bryant. Her commitment to the task is evident in her reflection:

First off I re-read "Thanatopsis" several times, taking notes and making observations on the actual work. Then I really read into the piece and began to reflect on it, preparing questions that I truly would like to ask the poet. From there I allowed my imagination to run away with me by setting myself in a small restaurant with this man and asking myself, "How would I make a conversation with him?" Despite all the preparation, it was difficult to animate Mr. Bryant because it is obvious that we have different views.

Throughout the paper I incorporated my own personal feelings on the issues addressed by Mr. Bryant. I allowed myself to become emotionally involved in what I was writing.

Since much of the work involved in completing the project was done independently, I became interested in learning more about how my students were approaching their tasks. I could see that they were doing far more than I had expected, and I wanted to know what process had led them to such excellence. I asked students to share how much time outside of class they had spent on a project and to explain what they had done during that time. One student wrote a narrative in the present tense to describe his process:

Walden. This is more complicated than I thought it would be. I need to take some notes to refer back to so that I do not need to read the entire passage again. The key idea seems to be simplicity. I'll have to find some specific examples.

Now that I've gone through most of the excerpts from *Walden,* let me take a look at his life. He certainly practiced what he preached, quitting a profitable job as a teacher because he was against beatings. He was a good friend of Ralph Waldo Emerson, who apparently had the same beliefs. I'll read some of his work later on.

Now that I have some background information, I can make good use of the library. I take better notes at home so I'll just copy some essays and go through them later. "Self Criticism" is twenty-two pages! Knowing how long it took me to get through that section of *Walden,* I'll set aside a large block of time to go through it all at once.

All right, it's the evening before the interview; so now would be a good time to review my information. I have found some inconsistencies and ideas that I personally do not agree with. I find it difficult to believe that someone who lived comfortably for most of his life could find so little value in the material world. I suppose I should ask about some of this at the interview.

This particular student was above average and very motivated. Because he could articulate the process so clearly, I was able to use some of his plan to help other students who did not have the same innate ability to chart their own courses.

I also asked students to read each other's papers and to discuss the kinds of things that others had done to reach higher levels on the rubrics. Their reflections led to whole-class discussions and one-on-one conferences that I used to make suggestions for more involvement or more effective use of time. It became apparent to all of us that the students who had started early had gotten help along the way; those who had waited until the last minute had performed less successfully because they had not had the opportunity to ask questions before handing in their projects. As a result of these discussions, students recognized that gathering more information, thinking through the presentation, and drafting the paper early enough to get assistance if necessary, would help them produce better projects. They saw how much more interesting some of their classmates' reports were, and they learned the value of hard work. One honors student took an honest look at her work and wrote:

> When I was doing research for this project I learned some facts I didn't know. Such as how seriously the Puritans took their relationship with God and how simple their lives were. I then wrote my paper incorporating my research into the story. When I was finished, I felt I had done a good job until I got my graded paper back. The grade wasn't that low, but as I started to read the papers of some of my classmates, I realized where I had made my mistake. I noticed that they had incorporated much more research than I had, enabling them to show a clearer image of the Puritan lifestyle. This helped their stories to have a more realistic tone and also showed they had a clear understanding of the Puritan lifestyle.

The Value of Ongoing and Varied Assessment Strategies

My perspective has changed completely over the past three years as a result of my experimentation with various forms of assessments, rubrics, authentic tasks, reflections, and portfolios. By looking more closely at my students' perceptions during the learning process, I have realized that often when students give me "the wrong answer" it is not because they aren't prepared but because they have drawn different conclusions about what they have read or heard. I have also learned that no matter how many times I "tell" students something, most of them won't remember it unless they have been actively involved in making sense of the content. Even students who truly understand a process can make small mistakes in carrying it out and thereby convince themselves they don't know what to do or how to do it. As a result of all that I have observed, I now view all my students, especially those who did not formerly seem involved, as more motivated, but also as more needy than I had thought.

This new insight has changed my role in the classroom as well as my attitude toward my students. Instead of telling students exactly what to know, I try to find out what they already know and what they want to know and then work from there. Instead of immediately telling them how to think or feel about what we read, I try to find out what they think. Then I help them support their conclusions or alter them based on real evidence. Instead of giving students a set procedure to follow for every task, I let them proceed on their own. I also help them monitor their own progress so that they learn how to complete tasks independently. In this sense, assessment has become an integral part of my instruction, a tool that allows me to meet the needs my students bring to the classroom. Most important, I now see assessment as an integral part of the learning opportunities that I provide for my students.

8

Realizing the Power of Reflection

Robin Grusko
edited by Diane Cunningham

If we ask our students to become reflective practitioners, then we must do so, too.

Robin Grusko

Robin Grusko joined the Hudson Valley Project as an experienced teacher of English and the coauthor of a book titled Becoming a Teacher: A Practical and Political Survival Guide. *Today, Robin continues to teach English in grades nine through twelve at White Plains High School and has just received a variance from New York State for a heterogeneous Regents portfolio class. Her involvement in the project has allowed her to become a leader in curriculum and assessment innovation in her school and district. She now conducts workshops on portfolio assessment, rubric development, and reflection. Recently, she led a workshop called "Reflection Across the Curriculum." Finally, Robin is working toward certification in administration and supervision at Fordham University.*

Robin Grusko's chapter illustrates what happens when a teacher practices and models reflection herself to teach students to reflect on their learning. It highlights the assumption that if assessments are going to extend and produce learning, then they must require students to self-assess, monitor, and reflect on their own progress. Robin clearly shows that the reflective process produces meaningful learning for her and her students.

Becoming a Reflective Practitioner

In the spring of 1993, I began my work with portfolios, unaware that a revolutionary change in my teaching, learning, and thinking was about to occur. I had heard of portfolios through various district workshops, I knew that the state of Vermont and the city of Pittsburgh had developed some fine models for assessments through portfolios, and I wanted to be part of the excitement. And so when my new chairperson introduced portfolios to my department—via the Pittsburgh and the Vermont models—I, along with a few other members of my department, created a portfolio for my classes. I see now that we were innocents in a land yet to be fully explored and discovered. I did not consider the outcomes I wanted the students to acquire, nor the various indicators that would measure whether or not my students had achieved those outcomes. That spring I truly "sprung" this portfolio on my students. They were not trained in reflection, nor were they familiar with rubrics. However, they approached the task with eagerness and created compilations of their work. I use the term *compilations* rather than *portfolios* because my students had not engaged in a reflective process. These early portfolios were really only poor prototypes for those that would follow. My students didn't create true portfolios until I became a member of the Hudson Valley Project.

During the first summer of the project, I wrote these questions in my journal: "How can I get my students to interact meaningfully/authentically with a piece of writing? How can that be measured and assessed?" By September, I had noted in my journal, "Is the portfolio merely product or is it process? It is process." Fundamentally, I knew that reflection was the primary difference between the portfolios I was developing in the project and those my students had compiled in the spring of 1993. It was a difference between the positivist, top-down approach and the constructivist approach. After creating my own portfolios based on specific outcomes during that first summer of the project, I realized that the key to using portfolios successfully was that the stakeholders—the students and the teachers—must make meaning through a process of creating, reflecting on, and evaluating that meaning.

This idea has made all the difference for me, and it is this idea that Giselle Martin-Kniep obviously understood. From the beginning, she asked the project faculty to become stakeholders, to make meaning of their own. Just as we were asking our students to put together portfolios, she asked us to create our own portfolios—a process that required self-reflection.

As a teacher, I had never really used a formal reflective process to analyze my own experiences. I had always promised myself that I would keep a journal, but those promises always seemed to go by the wayside. All of this changed when I joined the project. Now, almost three years later, it is apparent that if I had not taken up the practice of becoming reflective, if I had not been precise and analytical in thinking through my own learning, and if I had not zealously kept a journal to record my journey, my students and I would not have grown as we have.

Most important, if I had not been keeping my own portfolio, I would not have been able to understand my students' journeys. Accountability and ownership of the learning process are two reasons for our success with portfolio assessment. The reflective process was the medium through which this success became possible. If we ask our students to become reflective practitioners, then we must do so, too. Following is the story of the journey my students and I experienced as we became reflective practitioners together.

The Process of Reflection: Using Rubrics, Process Statements, and Reflection Questions

Without rubrics, our students cannot become the reflective practitioners they need to be. How can we ask students to produce work that is exemplary if we do not provide criteria for exemplary performances? How can we ask our students to move from mediocrity to excellence if we do not share with them the indicators of success? Before I became involved in the project, I had thought of rubrics only as summative grading tools, not as assessment tools that can be used throughout the students' learning process. But once I recognized the use of rubrics—and, in fact, once I began to see that assessment and grading are not necessarily the same thing—I began to use and develop rubrics wisely. Now, I do not know how to teach without them. The success of my experience with portfolio assessment is directly tied to my experience with rubric development.

I began my first year with a writing rubric, but during the fall and early winter, I became concerned that my rubric did not address the criteria of a good reading response. Students were providing summaries of the stories, poems, and chapters that they read, but they were not connecting with the work in a meaningful way. Fortunately, the enforced solitude of snow days enabled me to write a reader response rubric. My students were pleased; since September they had been writing reader responses with no way to measure the effectiveness of their work.

The following student reflection, written after the introduction to and use of the reader response rubric, attests to how valuable this rubric was for many of my students:

> January, 1994: This year, in English, I feel my skills have been sharpened, and my work has, on the whole improved greatly. I am now reading the novels more closely. . . . When I look back at my responses to The Scarlet Letter [the first novel that the class read], I am amazed at how vague they are, and how much they seem like plot summaries. If one were to compare them to my responses to The Red Badge of Courage, one would be amazed at the difference in quality, as well as quantity. . . . Self-criticism is an important skill, because it gives way to change and self-improvement.

During this same month, as I began to see my students' writing improve and the way that their use of rubrics guided their thinking about their writing, I wrote in my journal:

> January 25, 1994: I've been grading the midterm assessment essays, and I am really pleased. All the students feel that they have improved in their writing abilities—and in fact, their essays show this to be true, too. I have developed my research question finally: How does self-reflection aid a student in becoming a careful reader, writer, communicator? This is a really fascinating area of study. I need to speak to Giselle to ask her how I can research this in a finite manner. . . . Things seem to be coming together. Kids are really reacting well to my insistence on process. I'm pleased—writers are beginning to develop!

I was also coming to understand that my students needed more guidance in order to use these rubrics effectively. It was not enough to say, "OK, here is the writing rubric for this essay. Look at it. Think about how your writing fits on the rubric." I could see that I needed to get the kids actively involved, and so, out of my fascination with self-reflection and my desire to make the portfolio a success, the process statement was born. This became the backbone of my teaching and was to change the lens through which I taught and through which my students learned.

Process statements asked my students to analyze the process of the writing—to think about why they made the choices that they made; what the factors were for creating excellence; how they crafted their piece; and, after it was written, how they could make it better. I wanted students to understand that writing is a process—ever evolving and ever changing. I realized that my students would need specific guidelines, so we created these questions together to guide their reflections:

- How did I receive information for my essay?
- How did I organize the information?
- What was difficult for me?
- How will I resolve these difficulties in my next essay?
- Upon what can I improve? How can I improve?
- What can I do to make my writing better?
- What was easy for me? How can this continue?
- What do I know about my writing today that I didn't know before?
- How did I combat writer's block?
- Did I read it aloud?
- What are my areas for improvement?

These questions were the cornerstone of a newborn self-awareness. Initially my students were aghast at the idea that they could be considered real writers. They had been taught that only people like Ernest Hemingway or Robert Frost were writers. However, their reflections that year proved that they had started to see themselves as writers. And, as they became adept at their ability to use rubrics and to analyze their writing, I realized that this self-analysis through the use of rubrics, process statements, and reflection questions was the key to becoming a reflective practitioner. In my journal, I wrote, "It is not the portfolio that is important; rather, it is the process of compiling the portfolio that has had ramification for the students."

One student's reflection confirmed my thoughts:

> Mrs. Grusko's emphasis on processing has helped me improve my skills as a reader, writer, and thinker. As a reader, I have learned to pay more attention to, and look out for details and symbolism. . . . Where I used to briefly explain something without providing many supporting details, I now use quotes as well as more descriptive words, so that I express exactly what I feel. Commenting on the essay and doing revisions have helped me become a better writer, because I see exactly where my mistakes are, and how to avoid repeating them. . . . My thinking skills have improved in much the same way as my reading ability. Now, I often find myself drawing comparisons between past events and my current situation. Also, I pay more attention to things that I used to infer as being trivial, because I now realize that these slight details are often of great importance.

As I became more comfortable using rubrics I discovered another way to facilitate students' reflection and thinking. Two of my journal entries chronicle my continued thinking and learning connected to rubrics:

> June 12, 1995: When the pace is heavy and an individual rubric cannot be created, a good exemplar may serve. In fact, it may even be better than the rubric, because it demands of the students a different cognitive skill. Sharing an exemplar and asking your students to extrapolate from it the guidelines (standards) to which they must achieve demands a higher level of thinking than simply placing the rubric in front of them.

> July 1995: My growing awareness of the need to give students plainly-stated guidelines has changed the way I teach. If students are given—at the outset of a writing assignment—the goals they must achieve, they will strive to do so. Rubrics, however, are not the only medium we can use to help our students understand our expectations. I have learned to use exemplars to ask students to extract from them the standards that they need to reach in their own writing. Anchor Papers: They serve, too, to show kids the range of the performance they can achieve on the various levels of the rubrics.

Providing rubrics, exemplars, anchor papers, and guiding reflection helped my students understand their direction, focus, and achievement. The ownership we took over our learning led us to a real understanding of who we were and are as thinkers and learners. In fact, my students seemed to incorporate the very principles of self-reflection and self-analysis into their being once they were immersed in the process. Some of my students suddenly began to revise and rethink assiduously. They were really meeting with success; their self-esteem was rising, and so were their grades. In self-assessment essays written during January 1994, many students noted that the new techniques they were using in the class were helping them grow:

> I became a better writer when I entered Mrs. Grusko's class. I learned that there is never a final copy to an essay. When I received my assignments graded, I looked over what was wrong, corrected my mistakes and learned from each and every assignment. Learning is the basis of life besides that of having fun. Since there is no end to learning, that means the mind will live forever.

> Compared to the beginning of the year, my writing is clearer and more concise. The thing that has helped the most are the revisions. In the revision, I am able to clearly see where I have faulted, and I am then able to correct it. . . . Another thing that helps me are the self evaluation sheets we write. These allow me to think about where my essay is weak, or where there is strength.

Something revolutionary was occurring in my classroom. Students were thinking—and writing—of process, of revisions, of responses, of change. I began to wonder, Could portfolio assessment, with its emphasis on self-reflection, work with a heterogeneous population? In April 1994, I proposed to my chairperson that during the next school year I would take a group of heterogeneously grouped students through the portfolio process and on to the Regents examination.

My Venture into Heterogeneity

At that time, White Plains High School had a homogeneously grouped system of Regents and non-Regents classes. My proposal was accepted and a heterogeneous class was created. It had a carefully orchestrated mixture of twenty students of all ability levels; there was an extra period of English each day in the spring (a lab component) for every student; and a learning facilitator, Carolyn Tokson, was assigned to the extra period each day. Carolyn and I spoke throughout the summer and planned the course. Students would work in cooperative groupings. We felt that this would create a comfortable environment in which trust and respect would develop and nurture all those involved.

In September I embarked on my new journey with a group of twenty students, noting:

> September 19, 1994: These kids do not know what to say when I ask them to reflect on their baseline essays. We generated a list of questions: hard/easy? feelings? happy/sad with result? did I do well? Interesting, Everett said,

"How do I know if I did well? You didn't grade them." That opened up a whole new dialogue about the need for them to grade their own work and to self-reflect about their writing. I asked them to get to the least common denominators of their writing—the specifics. Before they reflected on their baseline essays, we read Jennifer's journal entry and asked each other how Jennifer could expand it.

It was clear at the start that my heterogeneous class needed substantial support. Carolyn and I labored that first quarter, helping kids come to grips with all of the new demands that we were placing on them. Getting students to revise and rethink their work was an extraordinary task. Never before had they been asked to think about their writing. My students would take the Regents examination in the spring, and since I was applying for a variance, their portfolios would become part of that instrument. We were playing for high stakes!

Teaching students who had never before been asked to respond to a piece of literature—save through the questions at the end of a story—also turned out to be an enormous task. To wean the students from the standard questions, I offered them the option of answering the questions or writing responses. I showed them exemplars, modeled my own responses for them, and discussed the rubric for the reading response. I was then shocked when only three students out of twenty wrote responses to the Bradstreet poem under discussion. Seventeen chose to answer the standard questions that appeared after the selection. I stopped the class and asked my students to explain. They replied, "It's easier to do questions because you really don't have to think; you just have to write it down. After you read, you have to reflect; then, you have to write. That's difficult." For these students, untutored in reflection and analysis, response writing was much more difficult than answering questions. The following month I noted,

> October 1994: Well, I returned the essays to the heterogeneous class today. We read an exemplary essay, and then I passed out their papers. I nearly passed out when I saw that they seemed unwilling to think. No one has asked these kids to reflect upon past efforts in hope of infusing the future with improved performances. It was like pulling teeth—without an anesthetic! Do these kids understand my intensity? This portfolio project is burning a hole in my heart! I so want the kids to understand, to take to this job of revision with accuracy and care and diligence. Am I reaching them? We'll see. I'll put on the board the following:
>
> Revision Plan: What will I do to revise? How will I go about it?
>
> My feelings now that the essay is graded . . .
>
> One thing I want Ms Grusko to know . . .

In November, I asked the students to write assessments of their progress in English. They were beginning to understand what we were asking them to do, and they were striving to achieve to our expectations. One non-native student wrote:

The essay that I am most proud of is the one about hypocrisy because I improved big time. Now, when I hand in my essays, I know I am going to get a good grade, maybe not an A, but a good grade. I hope that by the end of the year, my writing is the best that I can come up with. . . . I guess I am always afraid of papers and essays, because I still think of myself as the girl who couldn't speak English. When I had just arrived, and I was assigned papers to do, I was terrified because I didn't know how to write them. I would hand them in; I thought they were right, and I would get bad grades. I felt so frustrated and mad at myself because I didn't understand much. I still carry that fear with me, even though I can now speak the language and can understand things better. I hope that one day this fear will be replaced by confidence.

As Carolyn and I read the assessment essays, we realized that our students were coming to terms with the work that we expected of them and that our initial apprehensions about our students were unfounded. The grades that first quarter in the heterogeneous class were six A's, six B's, and seven C's; the fact that there were no D's or F's was a sure sign that the portfolio project, and its emphasis on reflection and processing, was having an enormous impact upon my students. The grade distribution in my homogeneous Regents class was also very gratifying: 9 A's, 7 B's, 2 C's, 1 D, and 1 F. In my Honors class, the distribution was as follows: 11 A's and 7 B's. Never before had the students in all my classes been so successful.

Analytical Thinkers Are Not Born; They Are Created

When I asked all of my classes to reflect upon their midyear achievements, students from the top levels to the bottom ranks exclaimed over their newfound ability to communicate. Here are the voices of three students who represent my honors, Regents, and heterogeneous classes respectively:

[Student #1:] My thinking is now on a higher level than it ever has been in my writing. . . . Jose Ortega y Gassett once said "Living is a constant process of deciding what we are going to do." As I have discovered this year, so is writing. It is a constant process. Never before have I been given the chance to revise my essays or other works. But this year, there is no "Final Draft". Nothing is final in writing. This has helped me greatly in my work, because I can always make it better, and see what I did wrong the first time . . .

For me, the big chore is always the same—how to begin a sentence, how to continue it, how to complete it" (Claude Simon). This is the way I felt about writing, coming into the year, but I have developed great confidence. At the beginning of the year, I felt overwhelmed at the pace and work involved with an English honors class. I felt scared, in class, and in my work. But that has changed . . . I now am not afraid to write what I think is correct, even if it is wrong. A lot of my confidence comes from knowing that there is no such thing as the perfect essay. If I am wrong, I can always revise it and make it better. A wrong interpretation of a text could be correct, since in English everyone has her/his own opinion, critics, teachers, and students. . . . My writing is mine, and I express my opinions and thoughts on my work, not someone else's interpretation of something . . . with my confidence has come enthusiasm for English, which I never had before.

[Student #2:] "One of the pleasantest things in this world is going on a journey" (William Hazlitt). My journey began with complete despair over my papers. It has been long and difficult with many bumps and pitfalls along the way, but I am slowly making my way toward my destination . . .

In the beginning of the year, my writing was terrible. My papers lacked structure; I had no organization, and I didn't know how to develop an idea. At first, my responses were trite, but I wrote often enough which made writing easier for me, and I soon came to understand my mistakes. I learned to organize my ideas and to state them clearly. Analyzing works was another high hurdle that I had to overcome. I have learned to look beyond the words for other meanings and the author's intent. Overcoming these difficulties has brought me a step farther in my journey to better writing.

I have written many papers and responses since that first day in September, and now writing comes to me more naturally. My responses have a sturdy base and are well supported. They are organized and have a specific message. I know how to express my thoughts in a readable, more organized fashion. I achieved this by learning the elements of writing. . . . Incorporating these rules into my essays is now second nature. Overall, my writing is much better; however there is still room for improvement.

[Student #3:] "One must never lose time in vainly regretting the past nor in complaining about changes which cause us discomfort, for improving is the very essence of life" (Anonymous).

In the past, I didn't like reading at all, and every once in a while, when I did read, I would just read and not bother to go over it, therefore, not understanding it. Now, when I am assigned to read something, I am also assigned to write a response. This makes me go back over the reading and write about what I think about it. This has helped my reading a lot, but what has also helped is going over the reading in class. In class, when we work in cooperative groups, I get to discuss the reading with my classmates. We help each other out by talking about the problems we may have had with the reading. At this point, reading is a lot easier and maybe a little enjoyable.

With every essay I write, my writing improves and I learn something different to improve upon for my next essay. In the past, I would write with many mechanical and grammatical mistakes, and I also had a problem with sentence structure. Now that I have written essays and have seen my mistakes, I know what to improve. In my essays now, I can fix my mechanical and grammatical mistakes. My sentence structure has also improved a lot.

All of the students who were involved in the very real portfolio culture in my classes began to recognize that learning was a journey, that there would be mistakes, and that it was all right for them to make such mistakes. This knowledge was helping them grow. Their realization that writing was a never-ending process and that revisions and self-analysis were part of that process was also helping them to achieve at high levels. Their growing sense of responsibility for and ownership of their own learning was clearly creating thinking individuals.

As Giselle stated at one of our sessions, "Reflection can be about products, processes, performances, knowledge, skills, and attitudes. It is best when it is specific, detailed, directed toward an audience who is valued, and purposeful. It requires modeling through rubrics, exemplars, honest feedback, and practice." By the end of the first two years, I had learned that analytical thinkers are not born; they are created.

Coming to Terms with "Less Is More"

The statement "Less is more" is an answer to a question with which I grappled for two years. By February of 1994, I had written the question down: How do I deal with the fact that students are writing fewer new essays, but they are writing revision after revision? I wasn't comfortable with the fact that my curriculum was not being covered as it had been in previous years. In the margin notes I asked myself, Does it matter? Although I was slowly coming to terms with the fact that writing revisions is more efficacious than simply creating new writings, I was still reluctant to give up the old ways. Indeed, in June of 1994, I had not fully done so. In my teaching portfolio, a portion of my letter to the reader notes:

> Quite frankly, my teaching has changed. For the better, I don't know. I have been concentrating on more and more writing activities, and I have been doing fewer novels and stories and poems. Is less more? I really don't know; I do know that time constraints certainly predispose us to validate the "less is more" philosophy. It is virtually impossible, if not actually impossible, to teach all the literature I did and do the kind of writing I want to do with the students. Something has to give. I do feel sad; this year, we did not have a chance to do Angelou's *I Know Why the Caged Bird Sings*. That was a loss, I do believe.

Another entry, written that summer, reads:

> I believe that I need to come to terms with authentic assessments; my thinking is coming closer to understanding why authenticity is necessary. The excitement of my students as they write their process statements is undeniable! Now that I think of this, their process statements are authentic assessments! I never really understood this until now! They have a stake in those state-

ments—and in fact, those midterm assessment essays, which they all wrote with such enthusiasm, are authentic. Case in point: I always administer a test for *The Red Badge of Courage*. This year, I did just that, even though I had asked them to write a series of letters from Henry to his mother, detailing the various points of his journey to self-discovery. The results on the test were abysmal! The results on the essay/letters were wonderful! On the letters, the kids reacted with excitement and understanding; the test's results were appalling! What do I make of this? I think that even the lower-level kids can produce high-quality work when given time to reflect, rethink, retool, etc. That is the benefit of this year for me and for my students!

By the close of the next year, I was clearly understanding the correlation between reflective practice and effective learning, teaching, and assessment. However, I continued to experience my unable-to-be-stilled discomfort with the fact that my students were not reading the same amount of material we had always covered before. My struggle with this issue is noted in my journal:

April 26, 1995: A Real Concern: Yesterday, when I began planning for the end of the year, I realized that this new emphasis on process writing has totally changed what I teach and how I teach! There are only 30 more teaching days left in the year, and we haven't read *The Glass Menagerie*. We haven't done the modern short story unit or the modern poetry unit or *Of Mice and Men*. I will be able to do the latter, but what about the short stories and the poetry?

July 5, 1995: I have found that there is no longer the time to do it all. Reflection and process writing has infiltrated my thinking, and hence, my students' work. I have found that "Less is more." However, I must admit that I am not totally comfortable with this concept, and I am still searching for ways to have my students read more. One thing that I have decided to do for next year, which may address this problem, is to try the thematic approach to American literature. This way, I will not be hemmed in by the time line of American letters, and I will perhaps be able to choose the novel, plays, stories by their worth, rather than by their place in history. Stay tuned.

And finally:

August 8, 1995: I have come to terms with my ambivalence. In terms of the curriculum: sadly, I have had to give up several units. I know that the Coalition of Essential Schools has as its motto, "Less is more," and although this has been met by the scornful comments of some of my colleagues, I find that it has validity. Of what use is it to read novel after novel, story after story without real reflection and thought? Why is it important that students know identities of characters and descriptions of symbols in any given piece of literature? Isn't it more important to ask students to reflect on their reading to establish a basis for their becoming lifelong readers? When was the last time an adult picked up a mystery novel and after reading it, had a test on the characters, metaphors, and similes? Yes, these literary terms are important, and they should be taught, but not in the context of 8 novels, 11 stories, 22 poems, 6 plays, and 1 biography or autobiography. And yes, I am sad about giving up some of the literature that I have always taught, but how effective was my teaching over the last few years? How many students read the Cliff's Notes, how many students merely read the last paragraphs of the stories, how many students just answered the questions at the end of the piece by looking over the story, how much of what I taught was really retained, how much of what I taught was really necessary for these young minds? Questions, questions, questions. Therefore, this coming year, I will be organizing—I hope, if I have time—the units in my American literature course in a thematic manner. In this way, I hope that I will be able to touch upon—albeit briefly— some of the aspects of the curriculum that I have had to give up: the Frost poem that I love, the Welty story that has an important message, etc., etc.

So here is the answer to the question: Are my students getting what they need to get in terms of the curriculum? Absolutely, they are getting what they need to become lifelong learners and lifelong readers. I truly believe that the emphasis on reflection and revision, along with the construct that less is more, has changed my students' learning and my teaching for the better.

Right before school began for the 1995–96 year, I constructed a thematic approach to my American literature course with five thematic constructs:

Searching for Self, Issues of Innocence and Growth

Facing the Barriers, Issues of Courage and Resilience

Coping with Relationships, Issues of Love and Loss

Living with Society, Issues of Good and Evil

Broadening the Imagination, Issues of Nature and Art

During each unit, students wrote one memoir, one literary essay, and one poem. In addition, students committed to writing an author project for the entire year, then writing a biographical piece, delivering a research paper, and giving an oral presentation to the class. I decided to try the thematic approach with only one of my American literature classes, and it worked well. I have since expanded my use of the thematic approach to my other classes.

The Habit of Reflection

The process by which my classes became immersed in a portfolio culture was critically important. The fact that my students knew—from day one—the outcomes and indicators to which they would be working was vital. My students delighted in the fact that I was learning with them, that I didn't hold all the answers, and that I could be flexible. Together we learned that self-analysis and reflection leads to the creation of thinking individuals.

I am not the same teacher I was when I first joined the project. Now, in any class, after any lesson, I automatically ask my students to process the day with me. I ask them questions like: What was important for you today? What wasn't as important? How can we improve upon what we learned and how we learned? What do we know about this that we didn't know yesterday? These questions are always forming in my mind, and this has truly changed who I am as an educator. My students, too, have seen the value of the habit of reflection. Their words attest to the power:

> One of the long term effects of processing is that now I always criticize my work without even thinking twice about it. I never hand anything in without looking it over or rewriting it. Not only did the portfolio project teach me about my writing, it has taught me about myself. . . . I think the portfolio project has given me more confidence in myself and my writing. The rubrics, reader responses, and revisions helped me to improve, and I am now finally impressed with my writing. I think the most important thing I learned is that there is always room for improvement. (Bonnie Hallerman, 12th grader, White Plains High School)

> Writing responses has been essential to me. A great moment for me was when I realized that responses were not just to say, "In this chapter, Hester Prynne goes . . ." but were to draw parallels to other books, find your own connections to a character or event, etc. For example, if you just sit down and read *Moby Dick* loosely, you may find it a bore, but if you respond to it, you will be able to make connections and actually find great comfort in the text. Writing responses really gave me a deeper appreciation of and a love of literature . . . I have seen how interesting and satisfying sticking with something and constantly working on it and improving it may be . . . I have gained more confidence in myself as a reader, writer, and thinker as a result of the portfolio project. . . . I have learned that it is good to take risks in my writing, and never to be afraid to explore a new idea, even if it is something I think I may not be "right" about. (Lauren Ambrose, 11th grader, White Plains High School)

> Processing my work has been a one-year experience which yielded results that will last a lifetime. It forced me to look at the necessary components of an essay and assess whether or not my essay contained these points. Having the chance to respond to any aspect of a piece of literature was a unique opportunity. I have become a more aware reader. Although I don't always write down my observations, reader responses trained me to glance deeper into a story, while reading it on my own. I still do this; even if looking deeper into a story doesn't help me in a class, it makes me feel personally successful. In general, revisions have given me the ability to improve, to write, and make the most of my talent as a writer . . . I have learned to question, think, answer, rethink, and do again. This can be applied to more than literature and five paragraph essays. It sounds funny, but it is a life philosophy.
> (Andrea Greenblatt-Harrison, 11th grader, White Plains High School)

9

Authentic Assessment at Work in a Self-Contained Classroom of Learning-Disabled Students

Jill Berkowicz and Diane Cunningham

I needed to make what I did in the classroom more meaningful for students and I needed assessments that would help *me* learn about *their* strengths and weaknesses in ways that traditional assessments could never do.

Jill Berkowicz

There is no doubt that a good teacher is flexible. A good assessor is also flexible and knows that her assessment repertoire should be flexible enough to meet the needs of all students.

Diane Cunningham

Jill Berkowicz is the principal of the Orville A. Todd Middle School in the Spackenkill UFSD in Poughkeepsie, New York. During her involvement in the Hudson Valley Portfolio Assessment Project, Jill was a special education teacher, an alternative assessment coordinator, and a Global Studies Regents Option team teacher in a junior/senior high school. In these roles Jill began learning more about alternative assessment practices. Her current responsibilities as principal, which include supervising instruction, developing new assessments, and supervising special education, allow Jill to continue the learning that started in the Hudson Valley Project. As she guides teachers in the development of curriculum and alternative assessments, she also encourages them to form a community of learners so that they can share their expertise as they develop new assessments and align their work with the New York State Standards.

Diane Cunningham is an educational consultant with Learner-Centered Initiatives. She leads short- and long-term staff development workshops for teachers about authentic assessment, portfolio assessment, and action research. Currently she cofacilitates several long-term projects with Giselle Martin-Kniep, including the Long Island Performance Assessment Project and the Center for the Study of Expertise in Teaching and Learning (CSETL). Diane has been using portfolio assessment for nine years with college students and with teachers. She began experimenting with portfolios in her writing classes and continues learning about this complex assessment system today, as she uses portfolios with teachers. She is convinced that portfolio assessment, and the reflection that it requires, holds tremendous potential for students. Diane has a background in elementary education and a master's degree in Writing from Northeastern University.

This coauthored chapter tells the story of Jill's first attempts to use portfolio assessment and authentic assessment in a self-contained classroom of middle school students. As Jill worked to make assessments in her classroom more meaningful for her students and adjusted her teaching and curriculum to meet their needs, she incorporated the critical attributes of authentic assessment taught in the Hudson Valley Project. Her story shows what authentic, responsive, and appropriate assessment looks like and highlights the need and value for learners—both students and teachers—to have opportunities to learn from peers within a community of learners.

Diane has annotated Jill's story. The annotations (which are indented and in smaller type) serve to highlight the attributes of authentic and appropriate assessment that Jill incorporated in her practice.

My students are distracted, social, unmotivated, confused, and misunderstood explosions of adolescence who are at the gateway of learning or failing for the rest of their lives. They are placed in my self-contained classes when their learning disabilities are so severe that they have been unable to progress enough in their basic skills to perform anywhere near their grade-level peers.

In some cases their intelligence quotient is extremely low and their accompanying behavior makes learning almost impossible, for them and for other students in the room. In spite of these limitations and because I love my students, I was looking for ways to interest, motivate, and challenge them. I could no longer bear walking into my classroom, looking at their faces, and teaching them information that had little or no meaning to them. I could no longer bear giving them meaningless quizzes and tests that they would either pass or fail, depending on factors far beyond their ability to report what they had learned, such as their ability to sit still for more than a few minutes, or their ability to obtain information. I needed to make what I did in the classroom more meaningful, and I needed assessments that would help me learn about my students' strengths and weaknesses in ways that traditional assessments could never do. And so I joined the Hudson Valley Portfolio Assessment Project.

The first step I took toward improving assessment in my classroom was to create an interdisciplinary course in which we used the social studies curriculum as the basis for most of the reading and writing curriculum. At first my students struggled to compartmentalize what we were doing. They would ask, "Is this reading or social studies?" When I explained that we were "reading *in* social studies" they were quite perplexed. They had been conditioned to see each activity they did as a "subject" with little or no relevance to the next "subject," and certainly with no relevance to their lives. However, as we began to develop connections between what we were reading, what we were studying, and what we were talking about in their lives, they became more engaged in their learning. They were able to talk about past and present issues, and they began to make significant connections between our collective past and their individual present.

> Notice that Jill's first step toward making her assessments more meaningful and valuable was to adjust her curriculum. Because authentic assessments are integrated, it is impossible to use them with curriculum that is not also integrated. Authentic assessments bring subject areas together and require students to use knowledge and skills from different disciplines, disciplines that our schools have unnaturally separated. In this case, Jill connected language arts and social studies in an effort to make both subjects more complete and meaningful for students.

As we worked with our new curriculum, I discovered that the opportunity to develop my students as writers was clearly missing. I had come to believe that writing is the best evidence of thinking. After doing some research about the scope and relationship between thinking and writing, I became determined to strengthen my students' abilities to think and write. I also realized that I could learn a lot more about them through their writing.

Jill's realization that writing must be a part of her assessment is critical. It reveals her new understanding that authentic assessments require students to communicate their understanding and learning. While the communication may be verbal, written, or artistic, whichever form it takes, it forces students to think and facilitates their learning.

The next step that I took was to design a student portfolio around reading and writing. I believed that this would be the most authentic way to assess my students within my new curriculum. The purpose of the portfolio was to document the progress of my students as readers and writers. Each portfolio contained a record sheet that noted the amount of time the student could read aloud or in silence, a record sheet that recorded the length of written work, and samples of the student's writing.

At the end of the year the portfolios revealed that my students were reading for longer periods of time and that they were writing more. However, the portfolio had meaning to only one person—me. My research question for the project was, Can I teach these challenged minds to think, organize their thoughts, and express themselves in writing? It was clear that the answer was yes, but I was dissatisfied because the portfolio was more like a series of record sheets than a purposeful collection of writing. I had developed a totally teacher-driven and teacher-directed portfolio that contained information that *I* wanted but provided absolutely no opportunity for students to choose the work to be included. *I* kept the portfolios—they had no meaning to the students since all of their work was used for my purposes.

At the end of that first year, I watched my colleagues in the Hudson Valley Project bring in portfolios filled with meaningful collections of students' work. They were meaningful because the students had been given the opportunity to choose the work they wanted included. I saw how that work spoke volumes about who the students were as learners, writers, thinkers, communicators, and problem solvers, and I was envious. I realized then that I had robbed my students of the opportunity to own their portfolios and to see their growth and successes. Had I allowed my students to choose their work, reflect on it, and look for their progress, the portfolios might have helped them to see themselves as developing writers with strengths as well as weaknesses. I knew then that I could no longer use a portfolio that was teacher-driven. I needed to come up with a portfolio design that would capture the best of what my students accomplished and that would show them how good they had become.

After a year of using portfolio assessment, Jill discovered that without reflection the portfolios had no meaning for students. All assessments, whether they are portfolios, performance assessments, or authentic assessments, should allow students opportunities to reflect on their products and processes. This metacognitive component helps students to assess their own strengths, weaknesses, and growth. Reflection enables them to come to know themselves in ways that will guide goal setting and move them toward becoming more independent learners.

At the same time, I realized that I had successfully helped my students to read and write more than I had ever imagined possible, and I wanted their written work to reflect who they were as thinkers. I had come to value written communication as a most important application of the thinking process and, as a teacher of learning-disabled and emotionally disturbed children, I needed to know that I could develop this skill in my students. They, more than most other children, act without thinking in ways we can understand, speak without thinking, and go through life without thinking. I realized that I could not teach thinking unless I gave my students multiple opportunities to revise their thinking. I could not teach thinking without making it visible and revisable. In short, I needed to teach the writing process.

> In almost all authentic learning experiences outside of schools, learners have the opportunity to rethink and revise. Whether we are learning to play golf, renovate a kitchen, raise a child, or use a computer, embedded in our learning are always opportunities to step back and think about what we did, what was right, and what was wrong. How else would we know when to try again, make adjustments, seek advice, rethink a plan, or take a step toward getting better? Writers, too, must step back, review their work, revise, and rewrite. They revise because someone, a real audience, must understand what they are trying to communicate. Clearly Jill realized that her students needed the very same opportunities to rethink and revise that all learners and writers need.

Armed with these realizations and with my growing understanding of authentic assessment and portfolio assessment, I was faced with designing a portfolio for a group of students who had great difficulty reading, who had no training in writing process, and who had been socialized into believing that they were not smart. How could I motivate them not only to think and write but to willingly revise their writing? As I conferred with my colleagues in the project, MaryAnn Bruck, a very talented middle school social studies teacher, described a magazine idea that had worked for her classes. I decided that I would replace the larger attempt at creating portfolios with an authentic assessment task, a magazine. Each student would write one magazine for each quarter. The magazines would be filled with their wonderful writing, and the assignments would be driven by the table of contents. I imagined that the first and last magazine would have similar contents so that comparisons could be made between the students' early and later work. To get started, I began assigning writing and gave each assignment as much meaning for my students as I could by always creating a real audience for them to write to: teachers of the past, students from their old schools, each other, and so on. I had a plan.

By mid-October, however, I was upset. I looked at what was happening in my students' developing magazines and realized that I had left a few things out of the plan. I forgot that my students are frequently absent, are often suspended, and occasionally speak to a counselor during my class. As a result, we didn't have sufficient time for sustained learning and continuity from session to session. Also, because each child's ability to produce was so different from the next, one child's magazine might be full and astounding while the next might be thin and depressing. Since I was very concerned with building my students' self-esteem, I had to create an assessment design that showcased each student's work, that would withstand factors that affected my students, and that supported my goal to help *all* of my students to see their strengths and their progress as learners.

At the same time I was dealing with another dilemma. This particular group of students was the most uncohesive group I had ever worked with. They had tremendous difficulty supporting and caring for each other. While they were all wonderful, fun, feisty, teachable kids, as a group they were tough to teach. I needed to help develop their vision of themselves as an interdependent and cooperative group. So, I revised my plans again and my assessment design went from four magazines to two, and from individual magazines to a group magazine. I continued to collect their work, study it, give individual coaching skills as needed, and return work for revision. If a student tired of revising, I would hold the paper for a month or two and then return it when the student seemed refreshed.

> By providing a real audience and purpose through the magazine, Jill provided a very good incentive for her students to revise. Authentic assessments have real audiences and purposes, beyond the teacher and beyond assessment. The magazine was a perfect replacement for a portfolio that would not work with a particular group of kids.
>
> There is no doubt that a good teacher is flexible. A good assessor is also flexible and knows that her assessment repertoire should be flexible enough to meet the needs of all students. Jill's realization that her four-magazine idea would not work because it could counter her efforts to bolster her students' self-esteem—and her decision to adjust it—not only demonstrate her ability to be flexible but also her ability to keep her students' needs in focus while attempting to document their achievement and growth.

In November, I entered their work on a computer and printed it out for their final edits. This was probably the most wonderful moment for all of us. My students had never seen their work printed. (I used my best skills to make it look very professional.) They read their own work over and over again. They read each other's work. They edited like mad. I was amazed at their motivation and willingness to revise their writing.

The first issue was printed in December. It took untold hours of my time at the computer, but it was most certainly worth it. The students were amazed and proud of what they had accomplished. As they read each other's work, no one made an issue of how long someone's piece was in comparison to another's. They did not make an issue of how many pieces one student contributed compared to another. They had all contributed to this, their collective work. They were bound by that common effort. As they continued through the rest of the year, they were more likely to take advantage of peer editing sessions. They were more likely to cheer each other on when they wrote. And, as evidenced in their second, final magazine, they were proud of how hard they had all worked. They had become a supportive, cooperative group of writers. More important, they had grown in their ability and willingness to write. Students who had barely expressed themselves in writing, who had disliked the effort necessary to write, and who had held no interest in revision, were writing and revising at the end of that year.

As we compiled the final magazine, I had students reflect on their work and write letters to the reader. These were included as the first section of the magazine and provided some insight into the students' thoughts on their experience as writers during the year. Although my students' pieces may not seem exemplary when compared to others, they are exemplary when compared to the work they had done earlier in the year. A closer look at one of my students, TP, highlights the value of the magazine project.

Like most students who think poorly of themselves in school, TP never saved her work. As soon as it was completed, goodness knows where it wound up. When I kept her work in a folder, she had her first experience to see it as a growing body. Her perfect attendance gave her the added opportunity to learn in a consistent manner, building each day on the next. My assignments to write and revise for the class magazine provided her with her first opportunity to develop skills consistently in Standard English.

Following is TP's first piece of writing for the year:

I don't like to write. I have nothing to say. I like to talk to my friends or write them letters. I don't like writing for school.

Compare this to her letter to the reader:

Dear Reader,

This is the best collection of my work because we can keep track of all the work we've done and see how well we've done in this whole year. What makes it my best work is that to see how much we have done. You put it all together and we count it all to see if we deserve to pass to go on to the 8th or not. This is my best work because I've been working hard since the time I've come to this school. I've been doing my best so I figure this is my best work. This magazine and the last is my best work. I feel that it is good making this magazine because it has shown how the whole class has done and how hard we've worked. My work in the magazine is good. I think so. Some of the stories I wrote are great and some you can say is OK. My favorite piece is prejudice because I think it is the best thing I wrote in the magazine. I also thought it was important that Mrs. B. told us about prejudice back in the days so that was my favorite.

The difference between these writings is dramatic, particularly in light of the process she engaged in. While TP's work shows growth, what is even more important is the fact that she has written much of her letter from the viewpoint of the collective "we." Her letter made me realize that the collective magazine had helped the class view themselves as a group. I learned here, as I did as a student in the Hudson Valley Project, that communities of learners improve education for all.

Jill's decision to switch from individual magazines to a collective magazine and the results that ensued highlight another important aspect of authentic and appropriate assessments. Authentic assessments allow students to learn within a community of learners even if projects or assignments are individual. Rarely does learning take place in isolation, and a goal of authentic assessment is to produce learning while measuring learning. Students should have opportunities to learn from each other. Jill learned about the value of communicating with her peers, sharing ideas, and problem-solving in the Hudson Valley Project. Her own needs to listen to her colleagues' ideas, to struggle along with them, to help them problem solve, and to feel that she was not alone, were and are her students' needs.

Through the Hudson Valley Project, I learned that the best way to develop any portfolio is in collaboration with colleagues who can be critical friends as well as sources of information and support. My collaboration with other special education teachers, English teachers, and social studies teachers helped me to understand the value of interdisciplinary studies but, most of all, helped me to develop my own skills at self-reflection. I developed a wonderful relationship with Dorothy Novogrodsky, another special educator who attended the project. We shared the same views of special education, we shared a thirst for knowledge, and, best of all, we respected each other. Although we have different talents, different experiences, and different styles of working with students and teachers, through our shared experiences in the Hudson Valley Project we grew as critical friends and came to rely on each other for support, understanding, and criticism. Without Dorothy's belief in my work and her support during my trials with my students, I do not believe I could have achieved as much with my students as I did.

My collaboration with Dorothy served as a first step for me. As I learned how to share my work with her, I began sharing my work with other colleagues. One by one I added more and more colleagues to my list of critical friends. I began to talk to others about their use of portfolios and authentic assessment. Outside the project, I expanded my collegial group. When my district asked me to share the work I was doing in the project in an in-service course, the course blossomed into a collegial circle of learners in our building. Teachers began to open up their classrooms as they asked each other about what they were doing and how they were doing it. Teachers began talking to each other, and, even more important, there was increased dialogue between special educators and regular educators.

My involvement in the Hudson Valley Project has changed me. As I became more comfortable sharing with other teachers and seeking their help and ideas, I became convinced that all teachers should have these opportunities. Further, I realized that what I found most valuable in the "classroom" of the Hudson Valley Project and what I now demand for myself in my work—being a part of a learning community—should be provided for all students, young, old, learning-disabled, gifted, or mainstream. This belief drives much of the work I do now as a school principal. My focus as I work with teachers in my school to develop new assessments and to align curriculum, instruction, and assessment with the New York State Standards is to create a learning community that will allow teachers to share their strengths and build on them—that will allow teachers to accept each other's weaknesses and work together to improve them. The most important part of my job is about empowering teachers to learn and share. I really believe that encouraging teacher-to-teacher sharing is the best way to meet the new demands that New York State has placed on us and to improve the teaching and learning in our schools. This is hard work, but my experiences in the Hudson Valley Project and the improved performance of my students lifted the burden of the effort this work demands. Truly, the hardest part was the initial learning, reflecting, and changing. Once the process became an integrated part of my teaching, the effort was less burdensome because students were engaged, proud, productive, cooperative, and happier. They were all of these things because they understood where I wanted them to go and how to get there.

10

Rising to the Challenge of High-Stakes Assessment

Julie Amodeo
edited by Diana Muxworthy Feige

I recall the day I began to question why.

Julie Amodeo

Julie Amodeo is presently an English language arts teacher at Marlboro High School in Marlboro, New York. She has been a secondary school teacher for twenty-one years—fifteen years at the middle school level and six years at the high school level. She served as Marlboro Middle School vice principal for three years. During the 1995–96 school year she was the recipient of the Excellence in Education Award granted by the New York State English Council.

Julie learned about portfolio assessment primarily from her participation in the Hudson Valley Portfolio Assessment Project and currently has a 100 percent variance from the State Education Department to use portfolios in lieu of the English Regents. Previously she served as writing coordinator for her district, and she now serves as the District Assessment Coordinator. Much of her attention now is dedicated to her work with the New York State Education Department developing the comprehensive English Regents that will be implemented in June 1999.

This chapter tells the story of Julie Amodeo, a teacher dedicated to providing her students with what she felt was the best education possible. Torn by competing educational goals—those of the New

*York State Education Department and Julie's own vision for her
students—she challenged herself and her students to re-envision
what could be rigorous and state-acceptable assessment measures.
Through the efforts of facilitators both in the state and the school,
Julie's story became one of shared growth and success. Ultimately,
the journey into the arena of alternative assessments, and
particularly portfolios, led not only to the reconciliation
of competing goals but also to the alignment of a
teacher's curriculum, instruction, and practices.*

Standardized tests. Regents. Final exams. The very mention of these words
strikes fear in the hearts of students and teachers. As a teacher of eleventh-
grade English in a state that requires students to pass a comprehensive exam
to receive a specific diploma, I know all too well what these words mean. I recall requesting that my students bring money for a Regents exam review
book. I recall devoting five weeks of precious class time to this review book
to ensure that my students were completely familiar with the test format and
questions. I recall grading endless practice essays from previous tests to set
the stage for June's test. I recall the day I began to question why.

Attending to Gnawing Questions

Students, teachers, school districts, parents, and state education departments
recognize the importance of student evaluation. However, often the assessments used are not only delivered out of context but are also multiple-choice
tests that do not demand any performance-based tasks or engage students in
higher-order thinking processes. Multiple-choice questions cannot accurately
yield the information needed to measure the abilities of students to analyze
and synthesize information, nor can on-demand timed essays truly convey the
processes students undergo as they write and read. These tests are prepared by
educators who have no knowledge of my specific daily classroom practices.
My students continually engage in the various steps of the writing process:
drafting, revising, editing, and so on. They respond to literature from a variety
of viewpoints, often setting their own focus and thesis. Multiple-choice tests
by no means adequately capture the dynamism of my students' learning; they
by no means ascertain my students' often sophisticated ability to interact with
literature or to communicate that interaction personally, analytically, and creatively. Consequently, I felt that it was absolutely necessary for me to pursue
forms of alternative assessment.

Many states and school systems are now moving to substitute standard-ized/norm-referenced multiple-choice tests with alternative forms of assess-ment that provide a better understanding of students' abilities to use knowledge, analyze information, and make decisions about their own learn-ing. Portfolios are emerging as a successful alternative form of assessment to promote higher standards, require students to become active participants in their own learning, and directly engage students and teachers collaboratively in the evaluation process. With portfolios, students often construct their own questions, reenvision answers, and discover ways of viewing their own work. These, for me, are the ultimate purposes of assessment.

And these were precisely the missing pieces in my instruction: measuring students' facility with complex knowledge, assessing students' growth over a period of time, conveying high expectations, matching curriculum with as-sessment, and enabling students to reflect on their own growth and achieve-ment. I wanted to move beyond the annoying mismatch between my teaching and standardized measures of learning. I wanted to find, instead, a match, an assessment philosophy and practice that complemented my teaching. This in-spired me to begin to create an end-of-the year assessment born out of the context of my classroom vitality and dynamism.

The First Steps

One day at a meeting of the Hudson Valley Project, the subject of obtaining variances from existing state exams was discussed as a method of alternative assessment. New York was piloting a project that would allow teachers to ap-ply for a 20 to 35 percent variance to replace certain sections of the state exam. This immediately drew my attention. It was a starting point to develop a form of alternative assessment that was more aligned with my classroom practices: the writing process, student-created tasks, a collaborative evalua-tion. Elated, I began to explore the process of becoming part of this project. I began a journey that would ultimately bring me to where I am now: using an alternative form of assessment directly woven into my classroom standards and practices.

With district support and my portfolio in hand, I attended a preliminary meeting for interested teachers who wanted to participate in the Regents op-tion plan. Representatives from the state education department (SED) dis-cussed the pilot project and reviewed the myriad of alternative assessments that had been developed. I was encouraged to proceed in the development of my portfolio, fine-tuning certain aspects. After a formal presentation to my board of education at an open meeting, I sent the portfolio and scoring rubrics to the state for approval. The turnaround time was quick, and my mission was accomplished. I had successfully substituted a portfolio with SED approval for 35 points on the state test, which eliminated the need for my students to complete the multiple-choice sections. Over a period of time, my students would prepare a portfolio of teacher-directed tasks as well as self-selected pieces and submit this for credit as part of their comprehensive exam. The portfolios contained the following pieces:

Portfolio Contents for 35 Percent Variance

1. *Table of Contents.*

2. *Letter to the Reviewer.* The students wrote a letter or other appropriate creative entry introducing the contents of the portfolio and the purpose of each entry. This letter was written in June after all of the other entries had been completed and compiled. (10 points)

3. *Author Project.* In October students selected an American author from a teacher-generated list to research and analyze.

    A. *Informative Paper.* Students conducted an extensive investigation into the life and time of the author. (5 points)

    B. *Critical Analysis.* Students read three to five works by the author and wrote a four-hundred- to five-hundred-word essay comparing and/or contrasting specific elements in the works. (10 points)

4. *Portrait of Myself as a Reader and Writer.* The portrait was an essay that showed that the students could reflect and analyze themselves as readers, writers, and thinkers. Using their baseline assessment piece written in September, their initial self-evaluation in September, their writing folders and response journals, and their exit assessment piece written in June, the students recognized their strengths and weaknesses and set goals for the future. (10 points)

5. *Reading Responses.* Students selected two reading responses written throughout the year and revised each selection to meet the criteria in the rubric. (5 points)

During the next few months, my two eleventh-grade English classes worked furiously to meet the expectations I had set for them. They knew the portfolio was a class requirement, but more important they knew that it was part was part of their Regents grade. More than once frustrations evoked questions and concerns:

Why do we have to do this? The Regents is easier.

With the Regents we only have to work for two or three hours. This is way too much work.

Nevertheless, the students surged ahead, realizing this was a reality. As the due date of the portfolio drew closer and closer, something surprising began to happen. Students became consumed with the project. Portfolio fever spread, and the students put their hearts and souls into completing this task. They began to compete to prepare the best portfolio. Time management was of the essence, so I directed my efforts in that direction. Classroom time was devoted to writing workshops. Students liked the idea of reflection. They liked the idea of being able to edit, revise, collaborate. One student was amazed that she could use a dictionary as she was writing in class. In the past this had meant cheating. When the due date arrived, all portfolios were submitted. My students had risen to the challenge.

Immediately I was faced with an enormous amount of reading and grading. The state required that more than one teacher rate the portfolios, so a colleague volunteered to evaluate them. The results were astounding. I had expected my students to meet the criteria in the rubrics as well as the standards that I had established. But these students had gone above and beyond the mere requirements. The portfolios were personalized representations of their educational pursuits. Beginning with the letters to the reader and ending with the portraits of themselves, their voices rang loud and clear. One student prepared her portfolio as an autobiography. Her letter to the reader was vivid and poignant:

Dear Reader,

This is the story of a girl struggling to grow up in a world that doesn't accept her. . . . While [her] name may seem insignificant now, one day it will be important. The most important thing for anyone to know about her is that she cares nothing for the biases of the world. If anyone tells her she can't do something for a minuscule reason like because she's a girl, she'll prove them wrong.

As a child, she was extremely smaller than anyone else. The reason for this is that she was born with a heart defect. There was hole in her heart that allowed deoxygenated blood to mix with the oxygenated blood. Due to the resulting deficiency of oxygen, her body couldn't produce the energy needed to grow.

Because of her condition, she had to have surgery. Without that surgery she would have died. This reality of the closeness of death has made her will that much stronger. Many people felt that because of her heart defect, she couldn't seriously play sports. How wrong they were! When she plays sports, it's a laugh in the face of death, and it's an act of rebellion against death and society. God gave her the ability to play and play she will to the glory of God.

If she had a dollar for each time someone told her she couldn't do something because of some dumb reason, she would be very rich. That amount of money would double if she had another dollar for every time she proved them wrong.

This book reveals to the reader her deepest thoughts and emotions. This book uses some of her actual writings to show the world who she is.

This student divided each entry into chapters. Extracts from her final chapter exhibits the intensity of her self-reflection:

How I learn is generally different than most people. I don't learn by listening to a teacher talk on and on. I learn by reading and by doing. This is why

I find school boring. The only real benefits I get from going is the pressure of having to do something, the interaction with different people, and the constructive criticism from my teachers. Often I end up not paying attention in class because most of my teachers just talk and talk. I am a very hyper kid, and if I'm not actually doing something teachers lose me.

Although I love to read and write, I have encountered some difficulties. The worst one I can think of is that I often had to put aside my other subjects to make sure I could get my English done. This disturbed my brain and my sleeping patterns. Sometimes it led to too much stress, and I thought I was going to die. It is a good thing that I had my friends there to listen to me and help me out.

The students had also designed covers to reflect their personalities and interests, and they had provided additional content explanations. They had added creative pieces to showcase their talents. It was amazing. Beautiful. The process had been successful. At last I thought I had found a viable alternative assessment that was woven into my instruction and provided comprehensive information on how my students learned and what they understood.

My students were still required to take the two written pieces of the state test: a literature essay and composition based on listening comprehension. After completing the written pieces, they were asked to respond to a questionnaire designed by the SED that asked the students to compare the test to the performance component of the portfolio. My students responded candidly:

The only thing that the Regents essay will tell is how I work under pressure. Writing shouldn't be a timed test like this. I feel that perfection in writing comes in time through many times of revision, like our portfolio.

Today's test is an uncomfortable, pressure-type atmosphere that inhibits the flow of your thoughts. I'd rather be home in my room free to think without pressure.

Today's test will tell you just about nothing. What does a listening comprehension prove? That I can listen? I always knew that! The essays are ridiculous. You need time to be able to write a rough draft, relax, and then go back to proofread and make a final copy. The test inaccurately evaluates your skills.

In essence, they felt the portfolio allowed them to demonstrate a full range of their abilities. Students also wrote that the state exam was easier and that the portfolio should be worth more than the deemed thirty-five points.

The Next Inevitable Steps

During that summer, the SED requested that participating districts in the 20 to 35 percent Regents option plan attend a summer conference to discuss their implemented alternative assessments. Educators from all across the state provided feedback. Like the students, they felt that the portfolio was far more meaningful than the exam:

> The portfolio was more authentic. It replaced very inauthentic, anachronistic parts of the Regents exam: vocabulary, spelling, and reading comprehension.

> The portfolio provided opportunities for the students to reflect upon their work.

They also believed that the amount of work required to complete the performance component was worth far more than 35 points. One teacher stated that it should be worth 100 points. I agreed and decided to request a 100 percent variance to replace the entire state exam.

The summer of 1994 was a busy one for me. In order to obtain a 100 percent variance I had to complete an extensive application. I knew that I had to refine my present portfolio. First, I reviewed my standards, keeping two that I had used in the regents 25 to 30 percent option plan:

> Standard 1: Students will react/interact with understanding to complex texts.

> Standard 2: Students will communicate effectively in a personal, analytical, and creative manner using oral and written language.

Then I added a third standard, focused on the reflection component of the portfolio:

> Standard 3: Students will be able to self-assess their reading and writing and establish goals based on this assessment.

All three standards were congruent with the state standards.

Next I developed indicators and tasks to enable students to meet these standards. In addition, I expanded the contents of the portfolio to reflect the standards. The required portfolio tasks were developed from specific classroom assignments. For example, the students study American literature in their junior year. In my classes they must select an author and complete an in-depth study of the author, the time period, and the author's works. Since this task requires the student to "react/interact with understanding to the author's works," as well as "communicate effectively both orally and in writing," this became part of the portfolio. Likewise, throughout the year my students were required to keep a reading response journal. Entries in this journal included teacher-initiated assignments and student-selected assignments that prompted student reaction to literature and literary analysis. Students used this vehicle to select those entries for the portfolio that they felt best represented them as critical readers, writers, and thinkers. All of the portfolio entries were an outgrowth of work completed during the year. The portfolios had to include the following:

Portfolio Contents for 100 Percent Variance

1. *Table of Contents.*

2. *Letter to the Reviewer.* The students wrote a letter or other appropriate creative piece introducing the contents of the portfolio and the purpose of each entry. This entry was written after all other entries have been completed and compiled. (10 points)

3. *Reading Responses.* Each quarter the student was required to write a reflective essay, 240–350 words, based on the current literature readings. Students were asked to respond to a character, a theme, a topic, etc., meeting the requirements of the reading response rubric. Students kept a reading response journal that formulated the basis for the reading response essay.

4. *Author Project.* Students selected an American author from a teacher-generated list to research and analyze.

   A. *Miniresearch paper.* The students researched the author's life and background to demonstrate a thorough understanding of the author and his or her works. This part of the project was completed during the first quarter. (10 points)

   B. *Critical Analysis.* Students read three to five works and wrote a four-hundred- to six-hundred-word essay comparing and/or contrasting specific elements in the works. (25 points)

   C. *Oral Presentation.* During the third quarter the students prepared presentations on their authors for the class. The presentation had to be at least five minutes in length and meet the specific criteria in the rubric. (10 points)

5. *Self-Selected Entries.* Students selected two entries from their class writing folder and provided in essay form a rationale for the selection. One entry had to indicate how the student revised to discover or clarify ideas and how the student refocused or refined ideas. This entry was written during the second half of the fourth quarter. (10 points)

6. *Portrait of Myself as a Reader, Writer, and Thinker.* The portrait was an essay that showed that the students were capable of analyzing themselves as readers, writers, and thinkers. Using their baseline assessment pieces written in September, initial self-evaluations, writing folders, response journals, and exit assessment pieces written in June, the students recognized their strengths and weaknesses and set goals for the future.

The 100 percent variance could not be submitted without the local board of education's approval. Consequently, at their September monthly meeting I made a formal presentation discussing the changes and the reasoning behind the new variance. Also at this memorable meeting, students who had participated in the 35 percent variance met with the board to discuss their portfolios:

the successes, advantages, and triumphs. The board was thoroughly impressed with their results and recognized the time and effort required to complete this rigorous task. Unanimously, they agreed to support the new variance and this new form of assessment. They approved additional time to allow for multiple rating and supported professional development to allow for teacher reflection and research. In December 1995, the SED approved the variance. We were on our way.

Initially, the students were excited and focused. We had started working on the portfolios in September. Yet as the year progressed and the demands of the tasks became more immediate, they began to hesitate. Once again, mumblings surfaced: "Wouldn't the Regents be easier?" "Do we really have to read all these works?" One student stormed the guidance office to sign out of my class. I knew this was a test case. There were other students who would follow in his footsteps if he was successful. Immediately after class, I called his parents and explained the situation. Fortunately, they were supportive, telling their son that if he wanted to go to the college of his choice he needed to exhibit himself as a diligent student. I silently applauded them.

Despite these complaints and mumblings, the students continued working. Many felt the pinch of last-minute due dates, but when June approached, portfolio fever was raging once again. This year's class was not only trying to surpass each other's work, they were also trying to surpass the previous class's work. Their genuine sense of ownership helped them to overcome their building anxiety, and once again the results were unbelievable. Portfolios emerged that reflected days of concentrated thought and effort. Students beamed with pride and they showed their portfolios all over the school. "I can't believe I actually did all this work," they exclaimed. "Look at my cover!" They knew they had risen to the challenge, met the requirements, and faced head-on the demanding standards.

Next we graded the portfolios. It was easier than the previous year because we had graded the author projects and the reading responses during the year; experience had taught us not to wait. All we had left to assess was the letter to the reviewer, the essay on self-selected pieces, and the self-portrait. Although the task was time consuming, it was enjoyable and certainly rewarding. We were reading pieces that were more substantive and meaningful than the prescribed essays found on the Regents. We were reading pieces that told the stories of readers, writers, and thinkers at work.

Unfortunately, the students were not done. The SED required that they take the two writing components on the Regents so we could compare the results from the previous year to this year. This presented a problem. The students knew they were being given the Regents credit for the portfolio, so how was I going to make them take these two essays seriously? Grade them for class credit. Students were told that the grades would be part of their fourth quarter averages. Realizing that these two essays would impact their fourth quarter grades, the students complied . . . reluctantly. They complained and groaned, especially on the evaluation forms they completed at the end of the Regents' essays. They made sure that once again the message was heard: "My portfolio best represents me as a reader, writer, and thinker!"

Regents Grades and Portfolio Grades

Some of my colleagues and the State were concerned that because the students were able to revise, redraft, edit, and seek input, the portfolio grades would be inflated. Quite the opposite happened. Four students failed the Regents because they either did not complete portions of the portfolio or did not submit one at all. At least two of these students would not have had any problem passing the exam. They were comfortable with short-term assessment tasks that could be completed in one sitting; long-term projects required them to provide too much commitment, dedication, and organization. They chose, instead, to prepare for the Regents exam in summer school. Many of the other students were disappointed with their final portfolio grade, expecting it to be much higher. However, after looking at the breakdown of their scores and focusing on their errors, they realized that they simply had not been sufficiently thoughtful.

During the summer, I charted each student's portfolio score, scores from the Regents essays, and class average (Figure 10–1). The chart shows that the portfolio grades are anything but inflated. Either they are comparable to the class average or they are lower. It is not valid to compare the Regents essays to the portfolios; one is an on-demand task and the other is a performance-based task.

Final Reflections

As I look over my journal, my lesson plans, and student portfolios from the past three years, I am awed by what I see. The changes are remarkable. My teaching methods and assessment practices are forever changed, and I know that the substance and form of that change will continue to be transformed. Regardless of whether or not I continue to teach with the 100 percent variance, portfolios will remain a part of my assessments. Rubrics will keep evolving, different incarnations with each task and each day that I gain deeper insights. In the 1996–1997 school year, for example, I aligned the rubrics with those that are being developed for the new English Regents. This match will continue to evolve, raise new questions, and provide rich possibilities.

The Hudson Valley Portfolio Project has also changed my outlook on education in general. I now know that there is no best way of doing things; a combination of approaches and tasks are needed to achieve my goals. I also realize the importance of using standards as a focus to develop tasks with specific guiding rubrics. Students need to know what is expected of them and to know the results of a year's worth of demanding, evocative work.

Figure 10–1
Comparison Chart of Portfolio Scores, Regents Essays, and Class Averages

Student	Portfolio Score/ 100 pts.	Literature Essay Score/ 25 pts.	Composition Score/ 30 pts.	Class Average
#1	77	17	25	91
#2	89	21	24	93
#3	81	21	26	89
#4	80	17	24	85
#5	91	20	28	93
#6	72	15	19	73
#7	77	21	27	89
#8	71	17	22	86
#9	78	17	22	78
#10	84	23	27	93
#11	83	20	25	93
#12	88	18	25	83
#13	89	17	27	94
#14	80	17	23	88
#15	94	23	27	95
#16	94	18	29	96
#17	71	15	24	88
#18	83	18	20	91
#19	37	17	21	80
#20	76	21	18	87
#21	94	22	27	95
#22	80	19	25	90
#23	78	17	22	87
#24	80	17	22	74
#25	86	19	26	93
#26	80	16	25	81
#27	75	18	24	85
#28	95	19	28	95
#29	98	23.5	28	97
#30	82	18	23	90
#31	70	18	23	66
#32	71	17	24	83
#33	70	18	21	80
#34	86	20	22	92
#35	75	20	25	89

continued

Figure 10–1
Continued

Student	Portfolio Score/ 100 pts.	Literature Essay Score/ 25 pts.	Composition Score/ 30 pts.	Class Average
#36	95	24	29	98
#37	84	21	25	92
#38	77	23	28	91
#39	85	19	26	94
#40	76	17	25	84
#41	94	23	28	95
#42	82	22	28	92
#43	72	21	25	91
#44	01	23	26	96
#45	24	18	25	58
#46	70	16	21	83
#47	93	21	26	95
#48	94	21	28	96
#49	90	21	19	94
#50	78	19	22	91
#51	74	15	19	83
#52	60	17	17	36
#53	93	20	25	94
#54	99	21	26	97
#55	72	11	25	79
#56	82	17	24	92
#57	75	21	22	89
#58	77	21	24	92
#59	77	17	24	91
#60	71	20	25	87
#61	76	16	22	71
#62	87	18	24	86
#63	65	15	20	74
#64	83	18	26	78
#65	82	17	25	90
#66	84	18	28	87
#67	69	23	26	80
#68	83	22	24	95
#69	77	19	24	85
#70	75	11	21	76

At times throughout this pilgrimage I would shake my head and say, "WHY? Why am I doing this? It was much easier before." Then a little voice would answer back, "No pain, no gain." In my heart of hearts, I knew that in order to ensure that my students had every opportunity to grow as readers, writers, and thinkers in meaningful ways, I needed to change my outlook. I needed patience, a certain amount of healthy stubbornness, flexibility, and on-going self-reflection. No longer could I be a disseminator of information. I needed to provoke, coax, and most of all coach my students in the learning process. I needed to come out from behind my teacher's desk and be a player. Like my students, I needed to rise to the challenge and meet my newly de-fined standards.

The story of the last three years is one that none of us will ever forget. It has changed our lives.

11

The Evolution of a Man with Dual Roles
Portrait of a Teacher and Administrator

Bill Peppiatt
edited by Diana Muxworthy Feige

I now realize that authentic assessment is at the heart of any and all these changes . . . This philosophical change has made a world of difference.

Bill Peppiatt

Bill Peppiatt's teaching and supervising career began in 1962. He has taught grades seven through twelve in New York and has supervised the English language arts program in New York's Copiague School District and Ramapo Central District, grades K–12. In the early 1970s, he served as vice principal of Highland Park High School in Dallas, Texas, while he completed his doctoral studies in Administration and Curriculum at the University of Texas. Bill is currently the supervisor of reading, language arts, and English in the Paramus, New Jersey, public school system. Although familiar with alternative assessment literature prior to the Hudson Valley Project, Bill had not implemented any of that knowledge until the project began. Since 1993, he has been active as a teacher of portfolio assessment with students and fellow teachers in New Jersey and New York.

The focus and direction of Bill Peppiatt's teaching and administration changed dramatically as a result of his involvement in the Hudson Valley Portfolio Assessment Project. It is clear in reading the following account of his three-year journey that the community of professionals involved in the project were vital to his redefined vision of education. Along the way, he added his own students to that community of learners from whom he gained insights, inspiration, and the courage to continue in what was often a chaotic struggle of redefining his vision and practices. Recognizing that assessment, curriculum, and instruction were instrinsically connected, Bill began to transform his teaching and administrative foci and practices.

From the outset I knew that my role in the Hudson Valley Project was different from any other participant's. I was both a teacher and an administrator. As Director of English and Language Arts for the Ramapo Central School District, I had been asked to lead a team that included two elementary school teachers and one middle school teacher to learn as much as we could about portfolio development and then offer staff development in Ramapo. And so I began a three-year professional adventure.

I changed significantly in both roles as a result of my involvement with the project. As a teacher, what I learned about authentic assessment and portfolio development dramatically changed my methods of teaching and assessing, my standards, my expectations, and my perceptions of students. As an administrator, what I learned about effective staff development from the successful Hudson Valley Project enabled me to draw from the model certain assumptions and practices and incorporate them into my own work as an administrator.

The experiences I had as a teacher in the project definitely influenced my behavior as an administrator and vice versa. In both roles I examined and re-examined critical, basic assumptions about the way students and teachers learn best. I have come to believe, for example, that teaching from experience is effective; that small steps are often the way we make progress; that we need to revisit concepts continually; that we cannot learn in isolation; that sharing and connecting is vital; and that we need to own our learning. These new commitments will be apparent in my story.

Changes in My Teaching Role

In the first year of the project, I taught one eleventh-grade honors English class at Suffern High School. In the second year I taught two classes, same grade and level. I decided to try a writing portfolio with my classes because writing was a priority in my teaching and a writing portfolio seemed very manageable.

Implementing Outcomes—My First Catalyst

The project began in April of 1993. One of our first activities was to try to understand the concept of outcomes and to identify writing outcomes for our students. Initially we worked in groups, trying to reach consensus about what it is we wanted students to accomplish in written composition. Soon each of us came up with a list of four or five outcomes. My outcomes included:

1. The students will engage in reflection and self-evaluation.
2. The students will communicate effectively in writing for a variety of purposes and audiences.
3. The students will demonstrate progress as writers.
4. The students will demonstrate respect and a willingness to participate within cooperative learning groups (peer groups) to assist in revising and editing pieces of writing.
5. The students will communicate in an individual voice.

These outcomes formed the cornerstone of my three-year saga. During the first two years, I revisited the outcomes in everything I did with respect to writing. One of the project documents defines outcomes as the "centerpoint for all alternative or authentic assessment processes." Nothing had ever impacted my teaching so much.

Because outcomes are student-centered and can be managed by students as they develop their portfolios, I continually asked them to revisit the outcomes as they self-assessed their own pieces. Before the project my students did not self-assess their writing, did not use rubrics, and did not refer continually to the outcomes for their own learning. How different I had become as a teacher of writing. How different they had become as writers.

The two outcomes I emphasized with my students were self-assessment and voice. Since this was the first time I had ever engaged students in the evaluation of their own writing on a formal basis, I wanted them to self-assess everything they wrote. I asked them to include the comments on the cover sheets for portfolio entries and refer to them in their end-of-the year final reflections. The theme for my class in this inaugural year of portfolio development—our implicit rallying call—was borrowed directly from the project: "The greatest power that portfolios possess is the power to bring the evaluation process to the level of the students themselves. Then, they can begin to develop and use criteria for recognizing quality in their own work." Quickly the students were adapting to this new self-assessment climate.

I had never been very successful in translating to my students the power and potential of voice. Therefore, it also became a focal outcome, one that we concentrated on throughout the school year. By the end of both years, I was thrilled with the students' ability to assess their progress in the use of voice in their writing. Review their final reflections, the last entry of their portfolios, and you will understand my delight.

Mike Wilson, a student in the first year of the portfolio project, wrote:

> Looking back at my earlier work, I notice two important things: a lack of voice and a considerable number of mechanical errors. Since then, however, I have drastically corrected these flaws. But I would have to say that the most significant change in my writing this year is my tone and voice. I have acquired more of a voice in my writing; these voices are always different. Just this past year, I have taken the voice of Holden Caulfield, of a high school kid submitting to peer influence, and of an obsessed old man who will do anything to possess his beloved. . . . There was a specific point in the year that I noticed the more details I added, the more alive the paper came. After I wrote *The Program*, my best piece, I became excited and my heart started beating faster; I felt as though it was happening as I was writing it. From then on, I realized what it took to be a writer. I had never known or seen this side of myself.

Skeeter Salcedo, a student in my second year in the project, won an Achievement Award in Writing from the National Council of Teachers of English based on some of the pieces from his portfolio. Skeeter's comments testify to his realization about the importance of voice in writing:

> Generally I find that my writing displays my growing appreciation and understanding of words and the language. I'm finding new ways of stringing my phrases together to make sentences do more justice to the ideas I'm trying to portray. I'm also finding it easier to find "just the right word" to get the job done. I still hold fast to my original anarchist approach to writing, but now I do rough drafts. I find rough drafts invaluable when it comes to seeing how stupid I can be and more importantly not letting anyone else see how stupid I can be . . .
>
> As I continue down the path of the writer I aim to concentrate on my editing abilities and shameless ignorance of the rudiments of grammar. I also want to refine my ability to choose words that simply go well together and effectively get my point across. Lastly, and most importantly, I plan to remain true to the style and voice I found in me this year—the voice that told me, "You're a writer."

Implementing Authentic Assessment—My Second Catalyst

Authentic assessment influenced my teaching more fundamentally than anything I had done in more than thirty years. It's true that I had been doing some authentic assessment over the years without knowing that's what it's called, but I had never deliberately evaluated my units of study using the attributes for authenticity. When I finally did conduct such an evaluation, I was upset with the results. Too much of what I did was still traditional, covering the curriculum but not coming close to authenticity. Upset but not deflated, I began to revise my teaching, making it more alive and meaningful.

Before I joined the project, my American literature course started with literature from the Puritan era and ended with selections from post–World War II. I followed a chronological progression. Now I had different eyes. I looked instead at themes, patterns, and connections. I sought varieties of learning experiences and ways for students to demonstrate what they knew and could do.

In an effort to incorporate more authenticity, I found myself asking the students on in-class timed essays not only to show their understanding but also to react on a personal level to the selections. On one level this part of the curriculum—essay tests on literature—remained the same, but on another level I tried to make these tests more authentic. I wanted the students to make more of a connection to the literature and to use their *own* voice, not their "essay voice." In a cover sheet for a portfolio entry on *Catcher in the Rye* that was written as an in-class essay, Skeeter wrote, "I like in particular how I went a little bit further into my understanding of the novel by extending the character I was exploring into my world, our world. This makes the novel that much better. The essay exudes 'me' all over the place."

I also decided to make an enormous shift in my teaching by using a writing workshop as a much more integral aspect of my teaching. The workshop embraced many of my goals, satisfied my five outcomes, and led to authentic learning and assessment.

I required students to write in their notebooks at least three times a week on any subject, in any genre. Several times a week they shared their notebook entries. I asked the students to select one entry and expand it into a finished composition. They gathered in peer groups to share their pieces and to evaluate them using a rubric the class had agreed upon. Zack, a student during the second year, wrote the following self-reflection:

> I like that it expresses how I really felt about running and racing. This piece is especially important to me not only because I feel I did a good job on it, but also because it was the first real, successful essay I've ever written. Sure, I've written others in the other grades, but nothing like this. This assignment made an everlasting impression on me, and a good one at that. As a result of this essay I was convinced that I could write fairly well, and it gave me a reason to try. I also like that Dr. P. read it for the class. This piece inspires me when I read it. Not many others do.

With each reflection, each collaborative sharing, and each personally meaningful task, my students were becoming self-critical, articulate writers. Again, as I changed, so did they. As I grew in my willingness to find opportunities that enabled them to exhibit and develop their talents as writers, they grew in their ability to learn from these opportunities.

The Murder Mystery/Research/Creative Writing Project, an idea borrowed from a 1978 NCTE publication, "Murder, Mischief and Mayhem: A Process for Creative Research Papers," by W. Keith Krauss, shows most pointedly my change from a teacher "covering the curriculum" to a professional looking for a way to infuse more authentic assessment. It was the turning point in my recognition of the power of authentic learning and assessment, and from that point on there was no turning back.

My objective in this task was to have my students use research for creative writing. I wanted them to grow as researchers and discover other venues for using research. In the first year of the project, I gave my students two options: they could use their research to retell the story of an actual murder in an original narrative style or they could present their research in a straightforward, traditional research paper, documented with a bibliography and citations. I was disappointed that only a few students chose the creative writing option. I also struggled to equate the two tasks in terms of difficulty and originality, a requirement for authentic options. In the second year (always changing and evolving!), I decided to make the creative writing task mandatory and more defined. The input from the second summer institute showed me how to make the assignment even more authentic by integrating the needed criteria of a real-life audience. Supposing that my students' mystery novels would be submitted to a publisher, I required them to prepare an outline of each chapters and to develop at least two chapters fully. In her final reflection, another student during my second year of the project, Amy, wrote:

> I rediscovered that writing can be fun when writing the murder mystery/research term paper. I enjoyed writing this paper because I had some good ideas. The week before the paper was due I spent all my free time writing, typing, rereading, and perfecting my story. I didn't mind spending all my time on it. Even though the paper had to be ten pages typed, I had no trouble reaching the desired length. . . . I know now that instead of forcing myself to write, I have to give myself time. I write better when I relax and let my story flow onto paper. I have to write when I feel like writing, not when a paper is due the next day, so I have to write. If I give myself time, I believe that I can continue to improve as a writer.

Implementing Rubrics—My Third Catalyst

Rubrics also had an enormous impact on my teaching, particularly on my perception of the role of students as partners in their learning. The use of a rubric was new to me in 1993. I had previously used checklists for grading, and I had used the criteria for evaluating the New York State fifth-grade writing test, but I did not internalize the power of a rubric until the project began.

First, hesitant and a bit frightened, I borrowed adapted versions of the Vermont Assessment Guide as a rubric. As the year continued, I ran into difficulty with the rubric, and my students and I started to create individual rubrics for the units and assignments. By the second and third year, I could not teach without rubrics. All of my standards and expectations became rooted in the rubrics, something I had never experienced before. And the rubrics, of course, were also part of the authentic assessment units that attempted to fulfill my outcomes. The use of rubrics led to exemplars and anchor papers, and so I was off in another direction. The seamless quality of the interconnections became more and more evident. Assessment was intrinsically connected to teaching and I, the teacher, was in the middle of a great tango.

The most exciting, if not revolutionary, switch for me, however, was involving my students in the creation of rubrics. I came to look upon them as partners in establishing the standards and expectations for the units. Our discussions about their learning, goals, frustrations, strengths, and weaknesses improved tremendously. Through the use of rubrics they were better able to evaluate their progress as writers and to develop ownership of their work. Revising and editing improved significantly throughout the year thanks to improved rubrics. I was also communicating with my students in writing conferences more efficienctly than ever before. Because the rubrics had enabled me to assign the evaluation of student writing to the students themselves, both in peer groups and in individual self-assessments, I was relieved of some of the paperwork and freed for more conferencing.

Freer and more focused, I was exhilarated by all that I saw happening around me. To my great surprise, rubrics had been a key to my evolution as a teacher. Most important, rubrics had changed my perception of the students and the relationship we shared. Partners-in-writing was our new way to operate.

Changes in My Administrative Role

The evolution that I experienced as a teacher inevitably affected my behaviors, practices, and attitudes as an administrator.

Implementing Staff Development—A First Lesson

The most obvious change in my role as an administrator is how I view and implement in-service staff development. Because I walked in the shoes of a teacher and designed my own teacher portfolio, I can anticipate how long it takes to understand fully the concepts of outcomes, rubrics, self-assessment, and authentic learning tasks. I know what it is like to begin a portfolio with a class of students. I know the joys and the struggles that will emerge, the dismay and exhilaration that can run rampant, the courage required to take risks, the patience essential to learn from mistakes. I can predict the questions and problems that might arise. As I work with staff development, I try to follow through with two practices modeled in the project: I take the time to answer every question that might arise, and I continually stress the importance of sharing experiences, materials, and uncertainties.

I also organize staff development around the critical, groundbreaking articulation of outcomes. As a teacher, I realize that thinking very deliberately about outcomes is the foundation for whatever follows. A solid portfolio design rests upon this understanding. When I was asked to write three to five outcomes for the writing portfolio, I had to review everything that I valued in writing instruction and focus upon what was essential and measurable. As an in-service leader, I consequently have placed priority on the identification of outcomes, following the successful pattern of instruction that I experienced in the project, by very slowly and methodically leading teachers over several weeks toward writing viable, measurable outcomes that they "own." I am now more patient than I otherwise might have been with teachers who are not moving as fast as I would wish in implementing their portfolios or who are trying new ideas. I understand firsthand how important it is for teachers to believe in concepts and approaches before they can use them in any meaningful manner.

Any number of teachers have asked if I could simply give them their outcomes or if they could just pull the outcomes out of a textbook or a prepared curriculum. My response has always been firm: avoiding the exercise of writing one's own outcomes is almost the same as saying that any writing folder is a portfolio. I do understand the temptation; I gave in to it during my first year in the project. Prepackaged outcomes, indicators, rubrics—whatever—are enticing, quick, and easy. Used as models to brainstorm and spark the self-discovery process, they are invaluable. Yet unaccompanied by a reflective design proccess they negate any possibility of ownership. They halt the necessary, though often chaotic, process of self-discovery, and they mask the power that emerges when teachers dig deeply to uncover their visions of how the students can develop. A successful portfolio must be as individual as the person who creates it.

In Ramapo, I was fortunate to work closely with the three colleagues who were also participants in the project, Harriet Yustein, a third-grade teacher; Audrey Verboys, a fifth-grade teacher; and Helen Lynch, a seventh-grade English and reading teacher. We met frequently in the first two years of the project to share concerns and progress, and to prepare for ongoing in-service sessions in which we as a team presented our portfolio experiences. Their fellowship was vital to me as I journeyed through the pleasures and frustrations of implementing a portfolio in my classes. All of the project's meetings provided opportunities for dialogue, which was often serious yet full of laughter as we grew comfortable laughing at ourselves. We pleaded for more regional meetings to increase our network of support.

The collegiality that developed over time was a lifeline, an essential ingredient in the success of our work. I therefore have also stressed with teachers in

my in-service sessions the desirability of having colleagues simultaneously involved in portfolio development with whom to share ideas, concerns, questions,
successes, and frustrations. In this way they can discover, as I did, the power of
true collegiality, the dynamism of working together toward a common goal.

Implementing New Habits—A Second Lesson

Some of our efforts in the elementary schools in the first two years of the project also had high stakes. Audrey Verboys, a fifth-grade teacher, and I worked
with her principal to design a variance to replace the New York State fifth-
grade writing test with portfolios. We acquired the variance and spent a year
working with the fifth-grade teachers and the principal, sharing what we knew
about portfolio development from the project. I did a similar in-service program and variance application with another elementary school that year; each
was very successful. Both principals wrote in their reports to the New York
State Education Department that the fifth-graders made significant progress in
writing as a result of their involvement in the portfolio project.

Harriet Yustein, a third-grade teacher, was even more daring. She worked
with her colleagues at Connor Elementary School to move from using report
cards to using portfolios and parent conferences exclusively. Of all our efforts
in the first two years, Harriet's were by far the most ambitious. Not only did
she have to instruct her colleagues in portfolio development in every subject,
but she also had to convince parents, administrators, and school board members that this was a better way.

Inspired by my colleagues' courage, I ventured into a fourth elementary
school. I met once or twice a month in the mornings before school began with
two or three teachers from every grade level and together we discussed portfolio development. It was with this group that I again learned to proceed
slowly and patiently as the teachers internalized the concepts and methods. I
frequently found myself repeating points I had made earlier as more and more
teachers accepted the use of portfolios. Some, as I had, needed to try out a
component before they became accepting.

Each of us approached the staff development differently, sometimes with
different objectives and results. We learned about the importance of having a
commitment at the local level with support from the central administrative
staff. We learned that each school proceeds differently also depending on the
principal and staff. Again, working with patience and faith in colleagues was
essential. We planted seeds that have had a lasting effect.

Implementing Staff Development in a New Venue—A Third Lesson

In late June of 1995, approximately two years after the Hudson Valley Portfolio Project began, I left Ramapo and became the district supervisor for reading and language arts in the Paramus, New Jersey, public school system.

Since I began in Paramus, I have been working with the performance assessment committee in Paramus High School, a committee comprised of approximately fifteen teachers from every discipline. Ironically, the two teachers who have made the most progress have not been English or language arts teachers. Cheryl Hopper, a first-year teacher in social studies, and Connie Story, a physical education teacher, have designed some truly authentic learning units in American history and project adventure respectively. For me, this was a first experience in staff development with teachers of subjects other than English and language arts. It was gratifying to see these teachers incorporating all of the concepts I had been presenting—outcomes, authentic learning design, self-assessment, and rubrics—into creative, unique units of instruction.

My understanding of educational reform and my role as an educational leader have also changed. When I look at the work of the performance assessment committee and other restructuring committees that concentrate on scheduling, the core curriculum, graduation requirements, and interdisciplinary education, I now realize that authentic assessment is at the heart of any and all of these changes. For example, a flexible schedule is more adaptable to tasks and projects that require more than one period in the day. Portfolio development, authentic learning tasks, and benchmarks shape the core curriculum and graduation requirements of a high school or district. Authentic assessment can only enhance any interdisciplinary curriculum. The seamless tango persists between instruction and assessment, and each day I move to its rhythm all the more smoothly, all the more committed. Each day I hear its power all the more clearly.

As an administrator (and, hopefully, educational leader), I have found that this philosophy has made a world of difference. I now have a sense of direction—a vision—that is far more precise. Whether I am interviewing candidates for teaching positions or setting goals for a curriculum, program, department, school, or district, I am concerned that authentic assessment and portfolio development receive top priority. It is my frame for moving into the future.

Concerns for the Present and Future

My story of change is an example of what is possible for both teachers and administrators. When I consider the progress I have made over for the past three years, I am more than satisfied that I was a part of the Hudson Valley Portfolio Project. Together as a community and alone as professionals we accomplished so much. I mark the project as one of the turning points in my career for which I will always be grateful. However, I am also somewhat anxious about the future of portfolio development and authentic assessment.

I am still frustrated that the implementation of portfolio development is proceeding at a snail's pace, especially at the high school level. I would hate to see this noble effort disappear like so many other attempts to improve our educational system. I firmly believe that teachers and administrators need to experiment with authentic assessment first and undergo significant staff development before they can succeed; some veteran teachers and administrators may need to be pushed to make this happen. To date, there are still many schools in which not everyone is involved.

Such cases require the leadership of a superintendent or an administrator who has attended a program similar to the Hudson Valley Project and who has gained the necessary sense of ownership and commitment. We need more administrators who are willing to reeducate themselves and to invest in long-term staff development.

Too many administrators direct teachers to become involved in authentic assessment and portfolio development without much fundamental involvement themselves. Their sincere, wholehearted involvement in understanding the value of authentic assessment and portfolio development is critical. The project made numerous attempts to involve administrators, not always successfully. Administrative participation often seemed shallow compared to the participation of the teachers who had been trying for months and years to implement the instruction and assessment. I suggest that if the Hudson Valley Project is ever replicated, administrators should team up with individual teachers to make the enterprise a dual responsibility; the administrator should also work with students. This would be an excellent use of administrative time.

Perhaps the push will come from the education departments at the state level; I sincerely believe that portfolio development and authentic assessment are vital keys to the success of American education. In Paramus we are fortunate that the superintendent and the board of education have embraced Strategic Quality Planning (SQP), a process for implementing curriculum instruments and assessment changes in schools, as a goal for this year and the next five. Through SQP, we have been able to make alternative assessment a high-priority strategy and action to enable our students to reach their intellectual and creative potential.

While the Hudson Valley Portfolio Project and the BOCES organizations have created a booklet containing examples of exemplary writing at each of the grade levels, not enough effort has taken place within the individual school districts to do the same. These exemplars are crucial for establishing benchmarks and outcomes for the future, and this activity would also bring about more consistency among the schools by establishing realistic standards at the local, state, and national levels. So many states have established core standards in the content areas, but we also need indicators of excellence to accompany these standards and collections of exemplary student work.

Finally, I am still concerned about grading issues—the Achilles' heel of assessment. Some of these grading concerns may never be resolved. Rubrics are absolutely necessary for any teaching we do, but in the minds of parents and administrators they can never replace grades. Should we place grades on rubrics? I have, but I feel guilty when I do this. Theoretically at least, portfolios make grades redundant. Until there is more understanding of portfolios and rubrics, grades will always be with us. One step forward, already taken by a variety of colleges, is to use portfolios as an integral part of the admissions process. Harriet Yustein's effort in the third grade at Connor Elementary School is one of the few attempts I know of in which portfolios and rubrics alone are used for reporting student progress to parents. I applaud her courage and tenacity and the openmindedness of the school community.

I have not spent much time discussing the role of parents in portfolio development mainly because I did not have many interactions about portfolios with my students' parents. I regret that I did not spend more time in this effort, especially when I became involved in applying for variances for state exams. As a secondary school teacher, I am not used to communicating with parents as much as elementary teachers do. This is my limitation, which I hope to indemnify. This is also something that we as a community of teachers need to change. If we increasingly use portfolios in place of or accompanying ondemand examinations, we must educate our public as to why they are far more substantive indicators of students' development and potential for ongoing progress.

With enough discussion, I am sure we'll find answers to these concerns. The Hudson Valley Portfolio Project has fostered a climate for this kind of dialogue. The readings, discussions, and sharing in the project made it a truly professional adventure, one I feel fortunate to have been part of. I suggest that it be viewed as a successful model for future staff development for local school districts or larger regions. More Hudson Valley Portfolio Projects are needed if my colleagues in education, especially fellow administrators, are to understand and commit to portfolio development and authentic assessment.

Transformation and evolution—if not revolution—is never easy. Its accompanying chaos is anathema. We resist it with a passion. Yet the status quo may in time be even more unsavory, more uncomfortable, and, for many of us, intolerable. I choose discomfort over compliance. My Hudson Valley Project colleagues gave me the courage to stand by that choice.

12

Understanding Teacher Change and Its Meaning

Giselle O. Martin-Kniep

I do not fully understand why some teachers actively seek to incorporate new learning into their teaching while others seem to avoid learning. Over the course of the Hudson Valley Project and other professional development programs in which I participated, I continued to be humbled by the complexity of professional change as an individual and social phenomenon. I realize that teachers encounter tremendous external and internal obstacles as they attempt to endorse new curriculum and assessment practices, even if these are fully supported by common sense and an extensive body of research. While some teachers' resistance to change is related to an inherent conflict between old and new beliefs and practices, other sources of resistance lie in the culture that surrounds teachers and supports inertia and current practice. The dynamics of change and nonchange involve the interplays between what teachers want and what they will do; what they believe in their hearts and what they espouse to others; and what they would like to imagine and what they choose to believe. The question that drives this is, How can we begin to understand the kinds of changes teachers go through as they seek to incorporate new knowledge and skills into their professional practices?

Throughout the Hudson Valley Project, we gathered information from different sources about teachers' thinking, teaching, and assessment practices. These sources included reflective journal entries completed during several of our programs or during our summer institutes and reflections and portfolio letters included in the teachers' professional portfolios. After examining the wealth of material we gathered, we concluded that the project had an impact on three major areas related to teachers' work: change in the ways in which teachers define their role with respect to their curriculum, instruction, and assessment-related knowledge and practice; change in the alignment of teachers' curriculum, instruction, and assessment practices; and, change in the nature of the work and responsibility that teachers assigned to their students.

I am not sure that it is possible to accurately depict the subtleties and intricacies of teacher change *and* describe such change in general terms. Whereas one can easily tease out salient patterns of change in the participating teachers, each of their journeys was a different one. As a compromise, I have chosen to use a number of letters and excerpts written by project participants in their second and third project years. These testimonials assert the primacy of their individual journeys and identify and discuss the salient characteristics of their change as a group.

Change in the Ways in Which Teachers' Define Their Role

This change is directed at one or more of three different areas:

1. Teachers' definition of themselves, with a shift from seeing themselves primarily as teachers to seeing themselves as both teachers and learners

2. Teachers' definition of their role outside the classroom, with a shift towards an increased interest in and willingness to work with, share with, and teach peers and other adults

3. Teachers' knowledge and sophistication as assessment developers

While not all HVPAP teachers mentioned all of these changes in the work we collected from them, all of them alluded to having experienced one or more of these changes over the course of the project.

Teacher-as-Learner

The change in the ways in which teachers define their role results from their increased awareness of themselves as learners and not just as teachers. Teachers act as learners when they accept that there isn't a universal answer to effective practice, when they recognize the difference between their convictions and their questions, and when they recognize that teaching and learning are in many ways mysterious. Neil Bright's letter is an exemplar of a teacher-as-learner. Neil has been a social studies teacher and director of curriculum, and is now an assistant superintendent. He reveals himself as a true learner in both his articulation of his limitations and in the powerful questions he raises about himself, about his students, and about assessment. I like the juxtaposition of his beliefs and his questions. His assertions reflect the value of process, rigor, practice, and depth in assessment. He also underscores the role that teachers play as models of practice for students. His questions, on the other hand, suggest an increasing concern about the meaning and validity of teachers' assessment and grading practices.

> Without any question, my experiences resulting from involvement in the HVPAP have greatly changed my assessment practices. A scant thirty

months ago, my theoretical knowledge of authentic instruction and assessment in general and portfolios in particular was nil. Although I was viewed by students, administrators, parents, and peers as an exceptional teacher, there was much about instruction I had never learned or had lost sight of since my teaching became corrupt by the largely stimulus-response nature of the New York State Regents exam. This "reinvention" of myself was humbling. After two decades in the classroom, I realized I knew virtually nothing about virtually everything. It was, however, also liberating in that realizing my ignorance released me to analyze who I had been, or what I had become. Such introspection led to the insight that in some ways I was a far better novice instructor with less content knowledge than I was an awarded esteemed veteran quoting discrete bits of information without thought and error.

As a déjà vu experience, I had been revisiting much of what I had forgotten as a teacher. Cooperative learning is again routine. Higher-level questioning and process writing are again the norm. Filtering instructional and assessment decisions through reality's lens is once more essential. Into this venerable yet potent mix of pedagogical techniques, I have introduced portfolios. While the value of these approaches are too numerous and perhaps too obvious to mention, there is one realization that for me seems most important. Slowly, almost fearfully, students conditioned as Pavlovian dogs to multiple-choice tuning forks have begun to risk evaluation, analysis, synthesis, and comparison. "What" has become "what if" and "true-false" has become "why." As I've opened myself up to new possibilities, my students have mirrored that courage. Thus, the greatest benefit of the Hudson Valley Project has been the realization that in freeing myself I have also emancipated those I had never intended to enslave.

Due to the approach of senility, and because I've internalized so many changes in assessment practices, it is difficult to document each pedagogical epiphany over the past three years. At the least, however, such changes would have to include the realization that . . .

1. In the number and types of writing genres teachers assign, less is more. That is, to evoke real quality in student writing, it is better to concentrate on fewer types and shorter entries but with greater repetition.

2. Trite but true, writing is indeed a process. High-quality student writing is unlikely, if not virtually impossible, in the typical on-demand settings found in many schools today.

3. Students can serve as "critical friend" editors for their peers and do an excellent job.

4. If we want kids to be writers, we must train them to model the process authors use to perfect their products.

5. It is essential to tell kids up front through models and rubrics what is expected instead of involving them in a "gotcha game" of evaluation after the fact.

Currently, my list of unanswered questions includes . . .

1. How much help is too much help? That is, when does student writing become my writing? Taken too far, assistance can lead to a situation where I am actually grading myself.

2. Are the reflections of my students truly honest or are they telling me what they think I want to hear in order to improve their grades?

3. Can writing enable students to think on a higher level after an assignment is complete? That is, can higher-level thinking be transferred to other non-related projects? Does higher-order thinking have any staying power?

4. Should an excellent essay written after three drafts be worth the same grade as an equally excellent essay that was exemplary at the first writing? If not, how might I differentiate the grades?

The combination of Neil's questions and assertions show the interplay of an increasingly sophisticated knowledge base about assessment coupled with profound questions about the role that teachers play in assessing the work of students. Neil's letter is an elegant demonstration of how wisdom is often accompanied by a greater tentativeness and tolerance for ambiguity.

Teacher as Facilitator Outside the Classroom

Many of the teachers expand upon their professional roles as they engage in ongoing and systematic efforts to work with other teachers. Teachers' appreciation for being able to work with peers lies, at least in part, in having the opportunity to understand their own value system and teaching practices and to further reflect upon their own thinking. This is a luxury that is scarce in the context of teachers' work life. As a result of their work with other teachers and with members of the administration, project participants gained a renewed appreciation for collegial endeavors and for facilitating their own peers' learning.

Debbie Glatt is a reading coordinator for her school district. Her letter is a powerful testimony to the importance of teachers' working collaboratively. It shows the synergistic effect of collaboration in terms of strengthening teachers' commitment and ability to teach effectively. She also shows that teachers can play a significant and perhaps irreplaceable role in supporting adult learning in schools.

Marilyn Sperber and I decided to share some of our knowledge with some of our school faculty. To our surprise twenty-two teachers signed up to take our first in-service course on Portfolio and Authentic Assessment. We called them Portfolio Pioneers and invited them to take a risk. As each teacher entered the room in which the training would take place we gave them a ticket that said "permission to take a risk." We were serious about taking this big step, trying something different, and really looking at what was said and done during the day with the students. While, as teachers, we all came to school ready to teach, we wondered about what and if our students were learning. How did we know learning was taking place? How did the students know? These were all questions that we would have to begin to think about. We told them that we were not experts. We told them that we were learning and on a journey ourselves. We wanted to build a community of learners to share ideas and to try new things.

Of course we had to give them the terminology, the articles, the models, the exemplary pieces, and the rubrics first. Before our first class we spent hours planning, sorting, talking, and organizing all the information we had accumulated. We talked about what had sold us on this new way of looking at kids. We knew the teachers would realize this would all be a lot of work but we wanted to make sure they would think it would be worth it.

Marilyn and I both agree that our participation in the Hudson Valley Project was most successful because we were two teachers from the elementary school building. We were able to work together, talk together, and help each other through the many stages we went through. . . . We have supported each other through periods of being confused, lost, overwhelmed, stimulated, and very excited. The benefits of our partnership in this project cannot be emphasized enough. It has had a positive effect on our school as well as our own teaching and learning. . . .

Several of the activities we did in our class were very successful. Each participant was given a puzzle to put together that reviewed the terms that are so essential to understand. Folders were compared to portfolios as we asked each teacher to make a list of attributes or possessions that told something about themselves. We then asked them to circle the ones that they would include it they were applying for a job as a teacher. The purpose of a meaningful collection of things became apparent. . . . Valuable time was spent reviewing samples of checklists, rubrics, reflection questions, and portfolios developed by other teachers. The time that was made available for teachers to meet who normally never get a chance to interact with each other due to different grade levels and subject areas was unique. Teachers were impressed with the fact that they could apply the same lesson in a different way to make it more appropriate for their students. They liked sharing ideas, hearing what teachers in other grade levels were doing, and learning from each other. One valuable insight that came out of these conversations was that there was not enough nonfiction writing being done in the primary grades. The focus of writing in grades one through three was on friendly letters and creative writing. No wonder the fourth graders had so much difficulty when they were assigned research reports.

Debbie's letter shows what is possible when teachers have a forum for rich conversations among themselves. I wish I could say that such forums are common in the schools where I work. Unfortunately, more often than not, the ways in which teachers can foster a culture for adult learning are limited to brief encounters in the hallways and to spontaneous sharing of successes or misfortunes among teachers or between teachers and other adults.

Increased Knowledge and Use of Alternative Assessment

Teachers' knowledge and use of assessment can change significantly as they begin to understand that assessment is more than a collection of tools for evaluating students' work. Increased knowledge of and proficiency with assessment are also associated with a growing understanding that good assessment should be diversified and appropriately matched to different and clearly defined targets.

The following letter, written by Pam Gatje, a fifth-grade teacher, illustrates her ongoing exploration of important questions about learning and assessment. In her letter Pam emphasizes that whereas some aspects of assessment are transportable, different students and classes demand the reinvention of old assessments or the complete creation of new ones. Her letter suggests a clear shift from a belief in curriculum as a relatively fixed and external entity to a process in which teachers select and develop learning experiences that closely match their outcomes and purposes for students' learning. She has also learned that three years is just about long enough to become comfortable with one's questions, and she has understood that answers always lead to further inquiry.

As a teacher-learner, I still find that my work often generates more questions than answers. For example, can it be possible that the tasks I'd designed for my former students were so great that they'd work for anybody? Or did they work only because they were authentic? Conversely, would the new tasks I'd created for my new students work on the old population? Or were they too tailor-made?

Early in the course of our training, it became evident that the portfolio must be tailored to a teacher's own class and needs. This became a reality for me this year when I changed to a new school with a completely different demographic makeup. The portfolio I had created was designed for the population I'd been used to working with. I was pleasantly surprised that the authentic assessment tasks worked well with my new students. I also discovered, however, that some things were missing, and found myself designing new tasks specifically for this group.

I find that it is becoming easier to design authentic tasks than it was at the beginning of the project. I'd been driven by publishing companies' ideas of how things should be taught. Now I feel guilty when I assign something that I know is not authentic. I have become more flexible in my curriculum choices. I have learned to take advantage of opportunities to motivate students by developing tasks that are based upon their interests at any given time.

The learning in my classroom is more project-oriented now, and although long periods of time are required to work on projects, the time involved is the same as it would be if the subjects were being taught in short, fragmented lessons. In comparing time spent on portfolio assessment to traditional ways, I think it is about the same. Planning takes more time, but the assessment is built into the task, so little separate time is spent on assessing the work.

I now have some preliminary empirical evidence to answer my research question, Do students learn more using portfolios than traditional assessment measures? I am giving a cautious "yes" answer based upon this year's New York State writing test results. My class this year had a 100 percent passing rate, with all but four students above the minimum reference point. This can be compared to my colleague's class, where three students failed the test and several others were at a minimum state reference point. Our class size and demographic makeup are identical. My class has more severe behavior problems. Despite this, my class outperformed his on the test. The only difference between our classes is that I used portfolios in my teaching of writing and he did not.

I have come a long way since my first summer institute. My portfolio is continuously evolving, and always will. My teaching will never be the same.

Pam speaks to an important consideration in the use of alternative assessment, namely a reutilization and investment of time. When teachers first encounter the possibility of using portfolios and other authentic forms of assessment, they worry about the time it takes to design, administer, and evaluate what appears to be more involved and complex tasks and measures. Because they see these assessments as an addition to everything they already do, they cannot imagine when they will find the necessary time to implement them. Pam's letter shows us that when we rethink our curriculum and instruction as we reconsider the assessments we use, we can use our time effectively without compromising the quality of our students' learning. In fact, whereas we might indeed invest more overall time in assessment, this investment is much more fulfilling in terms of students' achievement, motivation, and engagement than what we have done in the past.

Without doubt, the Hudson Valley Project program resulted in a greater knowledge and use of alternative assessment program participants. Their increased knowledge and understanding was most evident in their realization that assessment has many uses and purposes and that curriculum and assessment are necessarily interrelated. In some cases, teachers' increased sophistication led to restructuring classroom-related activities and processes, including time spent on different tasks. This allowed them to spend more time coaching individual students or monitoring group work, less time explaining performance criteria once the assessment experiences began, and less time grading students since much of the grading events would be shared with students. Teachers also reported having a greater appreciation for authentic learning experiences.

Overall, as teachers became more insightful about their understanding and use of assessment in general and of alternative forms of assessment in particular, they also realized how much more they need to know and understand. They also recognized that their learning, along with their assessment design activities, is a never-ending process rather than a series of finite events with clear beginnings and endings.

Changes in the Alignment of Teachers' Curriculum, Instruction, and Assessment Practices

Teachers demonstrate increased coherence in their curriculum, instruction, and assessment practices when there is a match among their intended goals for student learning, what they teach, how they enable students to learn, and what they collect as evidence of learning. This match can only occur when teachers develop a clarity about their intended purposes and can translate such clarity in ways that are evident in their practice.

Many of the Hudson Valley program activities revolved around helping teachers define learning outcomes for their students and use these outcomes as the basis for rethinking their curriculum and assessment practices. To assist teachers in the process of articulating their curriculum and assessments, we asked them to identify specific indicators for each outcome statement and to list learning and assessment activities that would elicit these indicators and their accompanying outcomes.

Lorraine Isaac is a middle school English teacher. The following excerpt from her portfolio letter indicates that she has used her exit outcomes as means to rethink and refine her teaching and assessment practices. Her use of outcomes as the basis for her curriculum and assessment design added rigor to her own standards for what constitutes good practice. It also enabled her to discard some of her lessons and to add new ones. Her writing also shows that all this work represents a significant investment of time and that she could use more time to further rethink her practice.

> Since I was designing an outcome-driven portfolio, my outcomes had to determine the assessments; in the past, I had sometimes worked backwards. Now I always ask myself "Why am I doing what I am doing?" This year I have rethought every task, and as a result, I have created better ones and eliminated those that did not specifically match an outcome. The fact that the students' portfolios will test whether or not these outcomes are met put a tremendous amount of pressure on me to focus on the outcomes all year long.
>
> The improvements this project has made did not come without a price, however. The amount of time I have invested in creating the design (I feel very strongly that a teacher must go through this process) is tremendous; and yet, it has not been nearly enough! Each time I attended a HVPAP session, I thought, "If I could have just one more productive day like this one, I'll be set." I feel that next year I will need twice as much time to make the necessary improvements!

Florence Manoff, a fourth-grade teacher, addresses the value of outcomes in terms of increasing the purposefulness of her teaching and assessment. Her excerpt also emphasizes the role that assessment can play in increasing parental participation and involvement in student assessment.

As the need to be able to show student achievement and growth in ways other than paper-and-pencil tests becomes obvious to all, portfolio development becomes a necessity, not an option. I have found that by using portfolios and performance assessment over time, my teaching has changed in many ways. One of the biggest changes is that I continue to question myself as to, "Why am I doing this?" and, "What do I want the children to come away with?" I have also given the students ownership and more responsibility. They help in writing the rubrics and can actually internalize good writing. Through their reflections I have developed a better insight into how students learn, write and think. I also feel that portfolios have enabled me to communicate with parents regarding their child's progress and writing abilities. Using portfolios at Parent-Teacher conferences has been helpful in sharing students' strengths and weaknesses in writing with their parents. I feel I really "know" the students as learners, which helps me with report card grades as well. Parental reflections and response forms have been very enlightening and supportive of this entire process.

Over time, most of the Hudson Valley Project teachers were able to use their exit outcomes as the basis for determining the merits of their curriculum; as the vehicle for increasing the congruence among their curriculum, instruction, and assessment practices; and as the impetus for developing focused and purposeful teaching units. Many also used outcomes and indicators to develop assessment criteria and rubrics for classroom assessments.

Our activities related to using outcomes and indicators were difficult for many teachers. Some had problems generating broad outcome statements and organizing their learning activities around them. This problem had a lot to do with the fact that teachers are used to implementing a curriculum they don't design and, therefore, bypass a consideration of the merits of such curriculum in terms of fostering their students' learning.

For other participants, outcome statements were too abstract and curriculum was a series of isolated and self-contained activities surrounded by behavioral objectives. For yet others, assessment was somebody else's business and didn't necessarily relate to what they most valued.

Without a doubt, this was the aspect of the project with which teachers struggled the most and took the longest to work through. It is probably fair to say that while all participants ended the program having gone through the motions of this process, not all were able to fully articulate and align their curriculum, instruction, and assessment practices by the end of the program.

Change in the Role that Students Play in the Classroom

Teachers demonstrate a shift toward learner-centered teaching when they recognize the inherent value of students' actively engaging in and, to some extent, controlling their own learning. This recognition is evident when students have a say in monitoring their own learning processes and achievements through opportunities for self-reflection and choice in how they approach teachers' assignments.

As teachers redefine their own role in the classroom they make a shift in the specific activities for which they ask their students to participate. Some of these activities revolve around helping students articulate their thinking and learning processes, while others relate to the identification of standards for quality work and criteria for student performance.

Betsy Flor, a fourth-grade teacher, and Joan Schlosser, a speech patholo-gist in Betsy's district, wrote the following letter to introduce their third-year portfolio. They maintain that portfolios are windows into students' deep and unique personal selves rather than assessments of students' learning. Betsy and Joan believe that students must have significant control over how they demonstrate their learning.

As with any form of authentic assessment, the development of a body of work that constitutes the portfolio rests gingerly in the hands of the student. To a large extent, the products created through the student's efforts are cho-sen with respect to the way in which they demonstrate proficiency on a given task or in a specified area, or pride in which the student was able to create something uniquely his own.

While draft work is also included in order to show growth, many of the final portfolio selections represent the benchmarks of intellectual achievement for that particular year in the life of the student. Frozen and preserved on paper or video or audio cassette is that student's reality of the moment and his or her impressions and interpretations that were brought to the learning opportunity.

The selections are like the pieces of an intricate puzzle that allow the reader to become personally involved with the student. "My most satisfying piece," "The piece I need to improve," "My explanatory essay," "My per-sonal narrative," "My living biography," "My poem." All of these puzzle pieces are in the hands of the reader. The reader constructs the portrait as he maneuvers each piece into the area in which it comfortably fits. The overall finished product is no longer the blank slate folder but a rich, vibrant exhibit that the student has created.

Even the evaluation of student work involves the students. If we are to teach anything, we must first have the students learn what we consider qual-ity and how to recognize this in student creations. The student invests him-self in the creation of the standard by discovering how to recognize and achieve it. Students become evaluators early on in their academic lives by virtue of all the material they are expected to comprehend. Each year they are in an academic program, they develop new standards for what they and their peers can accomplish. With portfolios, we have removed these previ-ously ambiguous parameters of quality from the shadows and allowed stu-dents to openly express what they feel constitutes quality in the area of communication. No longer are they told what the superior example is; they are actively invited to help determine what signifies excellence in their own terms. Through this process, we have actively engaged the learner and he has accepted the invitation. With such a personal commitment to the process, the student is empowered with a sense of newfound authority. It is in conjunction with this authority that the student brings his knowledge to what he will now produce. . . .

This program has provided great insight into the processes that learners go through when creating, revising, reflecting, and assessing what they have created and viewed. They have become shareholders in their educational experience. The emergence of the critical eye has changed the passive receptor of information to the active processor of information. We have become much more passionate about the issue of assessment not being relegated to the owners of an educational testing service who provide us with a tool in which to measure students who they do not know or appreciate. Their assessment tool often discriminates against the "square peg" segment of the student population that cannot fit their "round hole." Their tool does not help us, as teachers, determine the true intellectual growth of our students because it neglects to tell us how a student got from A to B. The portfolio gives us validation of that spurt.

Portfolios are rich and varied, providing us with a depth of knowledge about the learner. The assessment is continuous, rather than reserved for that momentary testing situation. Assessment is an area where our learners need to know what is expected of them, in order for them to be partners in the educational forum.

Joanne Anderson is a middle school teacher who teaches English. Her excerpt presents a number of arguments in support of letting students assume responsibility for their learning. First, she writes about the importance and impact of students seeing and discussing exemplary work as the basis for understanding evaluation criteria. Second, she emphasizes that when students have a say in how they approach a writing task—and even in what they write about—they produce better and more engaging writing. Third, she understands that in order to give students control over what and how they are learning, she must be flexible instead of demanding that students follow specific timelines to demonstrate their learning. Finally, Joanne reminds us of the need to create a variety of assessments to support the many different ways that students learn.

Prior to my involvement with the project, I assessed my students in the traditional way that I had done for years. I was still pretty much entrenched in the notion of teaching a particular writing strategy, assigning a topic, and marking the paper with my red pen. It never occurred to me to share exemplars with my students prior to their completion of a task, nor did it occur to me to ask students to think about their writing or to reflect on their assignments. I

believed pretty much like my students that once I returned their graded paper that was the end of it.

This project has lent credence to what I've been pioneering over the
course of the year. My teaching practices have changed to include process
writing and writer's workshop. I have come to realize that students do better
when they select the topics about which they are going to write. There has
been a decided shift in my classroom to an emphasis on reading and writing.

I have realized the importance of providing my students with exemplars. They need to know ahead of time what an "A" paper looks like. Thus,
I have begun collecting exemplars from past work and have even provided
them myself when necessary. My students write about four times per week,
and they read an average of one novel a month. I have also come to realize
that we all don't have to read the same novel and be on the same page. Over
the course of the year my students have self-selected the novels they have
read. Some months it was a free-choice selection, and other months they
self-selected a novel from a particular genre I had designated. They always
had the opportunity to select another title if they were not pleased with their
first choice. I learned that students can be very honest and insightful when
asked to evaluate and reflect on their writing.

I have also learned that if I value an assignment I need to provide my
students with time so that they can do their best work. Students need to be
assessed/evaluated in a variety of ways. A test is like a snapshot capturing a
student's performance at one moment in time. A portfolio is like a photo al-
bum measuring a student's work over time. Finally, I learned that I am still
learning.

Margaret Brizzie, a sixth-grade teacher, wrote an excerpt that highlights
the transformation of her role as well as of her students' role. Such transformation was not only rewarding in terms of the investments that students made
in their learning but also in the validation of her role as a facilitator.

As writers attempted writing tasks armed with rubrics and the knowledge
that they would be "in charge" of their writing portfolios and selections, two
things happened. Students exhibited a marked increase in interest and motivation to do writing (and seriously work at it), and much of the burden
shifted from teacher to student.

My teaching practices became validated in a very short time. A relaxed,
even more student-focused classroom environment prevailed. I took on a
role that put me into a lot of behind-the-scenes preparation, took me away
from my desk and made me a nomad; and my expectations of my students
grew tremendously. Although I have always been a very well-planned,
packing-every-minute kind of teacher, and that has remained the same, my
role has changed. More class time is controlled by students' working, re-
searching, collaborating, planning, designing, and writing. I am the assem-
bler of materials, a resource for possible directions to go, arranging for the

library or computer room or an alternative work space. I conference with one or more people or small groups. I design unobtrusive checkup self-assessments to "drop in" on progress of a task or project so as to foster continuity of a student's time on task. I observe, monitor, and then give feedback on the in-progress works.

Students have improved their own self-control not only in the completion of tasks but in behavior, learning, and working style, individual needs, and interdependence. The classroom is always buzzing but it is a relaxing, educational hum. We are more approachable equals in this environment. My hope is that I can remember how we began so next year we can achieve similar growth, both personally and academically.

Students emerge with many more dimensions and they appear to be more aware of their own changes. Works are not dismissed as grades. No one seems as competitive because we talk much more about efforts. (Higher-caliber students took more time to relax about less emphasis on grades.) Generally, all students, no matter what their capabilities, know if they put forth their best or adequate efforts. Honesty in the assessment of their own work or that of others was apparent.

Students cannot only do more in the context of authentic tasks, using rubrics describing specific expectations, practicing self- or conference assessment tools, but they are more motivated and are truly a greater part of the process. Actually now they are an integral part of the process. The burden has shifted. I no longer plan the lesson, teach it, receive the assignment, read it, grade it, give feedback on revisions, make certain revisions happen, and regrade. Now students understand the tasks, do further research, complete them, self-assess them, revise, get peer or teacher feedback, and submit them in their more final form.

In looking at changes in teachers' involvement of students in their own learning, teachers emphasize the relationship between students' articulation of their learning process and an increase in both teachers' and students' metacognition. In addition to paying increased attention to students' thinking and learning processes, teachers involve students in identifying criteria to assess their own performance, selecting specific activities or work to document their learning, and evaluating their work and that of their peers.

It is noteworthy that of all the project teachers who wrote about the discrepancy between their expectations for students' work and what students actually produced, none of them indicated that they originally expected more from students than what their students were able to accomplish. When teachers began their work in the project, they had great difficulties accepting the value of using outside models and exemplars as the basis for the construction of rubrics and grading criteria. In particular, they worried about students' becoming frustrated or giving up on their efforts because standards would be too high for them to reach. In fact, none of the teachers reported that this problem actually happened.

I have chosen an essay written by Tom Kersting, a high school English teacher, as the final example of teacher change. Tom is a wonderful thinker and writer. His essay demonstrates his deep understanding of the value of assessment as a dynamic process that mirrors his own development as an assessor and his willingness to share the control over learning with his students. Tom is aware that he can use portfolio assessment as a window into students' uniqueness—that is, to discover and even celebrate each of his students' accomplishments and growth. Students choose how to engage with assignments and enjoy opportunities to engage with them personally.

So How Does My Garden Grow?

I'm currently cultivating a wildflower garden in a 6' × 15' patch of soil just before the stone wall at the back of our yard. I've been considering such a garden for quite some time now, despite the comfortable aesthetic appeal of the backyard landscape and its proportions: to the right the deck, the pool, the rock garden we have sculpted over the years, its entry graced by a cedar arbor—all balanced by a line of ash, black cherry, and silver maple arrayed like sentinels to the left, with the weed-free, disciplined rows of the vegetable garden just beyond.

Colors bursting forth in spring, fragrant with the redolence of lilac and honeysuckle, the yard had over the years become a haven for hosts of native songbirds, nature with its panoply of sights and sounds and smells. But something was missing. It was a programmed landscape tamed and snipped and trimmed as lovely as the lawn. It was my version of nature carefully controlled for its aesthetic appeal, allowed to sprout its glory only insofar as it fit my scheme of things: it was nature on my terms, nature contained. What was needed, I sensed, was the lush, untutored defiance of a wildflower garden.

And so I have planted my garden of wildflowers at center stage in the back of the yard, and it has reminded me ever since of my work with portfolios and other forms of authentic assessment. As with portfolio work, there's much about the garden that's beyond my control. Having carefully prepared the soil, sown the seeds, tamped down the earth, and watered faithfully for a week, I wait and watch and hope and coax the seedlings as they grope toward the nurturing sun.

This morning I stood awhile on the fringe of the garden appraising its progress since yesterday. Over the low drone of the pool filter the finches were chirping a morning medley and a slight breeze nudged from the canopy overhead a flurry of drips from last night's storm. Quite suddenly then, a foot away at the front of the garden, I saw the earth heave as a tunnel rose just beneath the surface. I was stunned for a moment, until I realized I had witnessed the excavations of a mole on the morning shift. I tapped his tunnel with the edge of a hoe in hopes of driving the intruder from beneath my garden, knowing full well that I'd more likely succeeded in driving him to burrow deeper.

So much is beyond our control. I noticed today several bald patches near the front of the garden. I thought I had sown the seeds more evenly. The seedlings that are sprouting now are mere millimeters tall, some yearning toward inches. I have no control over how many or which will transform themselves into bounteous wildflowers, or when this miracle will occur. I have no control over the immune systems of the various flowers in the mix, or of the diseases lurking in the soil or air. I have, in short, no control over how my garden will grow, but I know that if I continue to water it and contend with the moles, I will have done all that I can do to assure that it grows, each wildflower reaching toward its full resplendent potential. I live on hope.

And so it is with my students and their work with portfolios. Part of the beauty of planting a wildflower garden is that you never really know what it's going to produce, and so every day yields a surprise. Scattered about in random clusters, the poppies and daisies, larkspurs, bluebonnets, and snapdragons display their best features to the light of the sun. So, too, with my students as they strive toward their potential in the portfolio process. I sow seeds of possibility, set certain borders, certain parameters within which they may operate, occasionally spook the moles and other distractors in hopes that fertile ideas will germinate, take root, and flourish. Some of their ideas and efforts will be pecked away by the birds, some I will step on inadvertently, still others will sprout only to wilt and wither. But each little failure provides space for other seedlings to grow and to bloom. Yet, as with my students' portfolios, the wildflowers will not all blossom at the same time, or even in the same season. As if to mirror the diversity among my students' interests and abilities, some are resplendent in the afternoon sunlight, others more comely in the evening shade. The degree to which I am mindful of such diversity is one measure of my success; the degree to which I have forgotten it, a measure of my failure.

A curious feature of a wildflower garden is that no one can tell which seedling is a wildflower and which a weed. "A weed," Emerson once wrote, "is just a wildflower, the beauty of which is yet to be discovered." There are many weeds out there that we simply don't appreciate yet. Given conditions that foster individual performance and design within a context that values what they may produce, many of my students will sprout the most wondrous weeds. My efforts at alternative assessment are helping me to discover their beauty. Within the borders of the garden, I can value them as the wildflowers that they are. As with cultivating a wildflower garden, my work with portfolios and other forms of authentic assessment has been about letting go of control, nurturing the growth, and celebrating the beauty that blossoms.

Tom's essay highlights the paradoxes involved in using assessment to both support and measure learning. It is so difficult for teachers to accept the tensions involved in being advocates for individual growth and achievement while at the same time being responsible for getting students to a common place in a predefined amount of time. Furthermore, many teachers have difficulty finding a balance between authentic learning experiences and other curriculum- and assessment-related activities that are more closely connected to high-stakes assessment or to the formal curriculum. This balance is particularly difficult to reach when schools districts and state departments of education issue mixed messages about the direction curriculum and assessment should take.

Unresolved and Difficult Questions

There is no such thing as absolute success in staff development. While there is no question that the Hudson Valley Project offered teachers opportunities for growth and inquiry, it did not reach all teachers to the same extent. Teachers' knowledge base, expectations, work conditions, and needs were as different as those found in any classroom. Some teachers came to us knowing much about alternative assessment and about learner-centered pedagogy; others arrived with little prior knowledge in these areas or with little support in their schools for such knowledge and skills.

One of the important lessons I have learned from teachers, especially from those who left the program, is that teachers often have extremely high and unreasonable standards for their own learning, along with a very low tolerance for making mistakes. While many teachers are able to move past a state of dissonance and discomfort, not all teachers are able to reconcile new learning with their existing practices.

Carolyn Bagley is a first-grade teacher who left the project at the end of her second year. Like many other teachers in the project, Carolyn struggled to fit her work into what she believed was expected of her. Throughout her participation in the project, she was uncomfortable with not having a neat and completed assessment package; yet she also realized, perhaps earlier than most teachers in the project, that it's not possible to change one's assessment without a willingness to reconsider and even change one's curriculum and instructional practices.

Carolyn also depicts a particular phenomenon related to teachers' learning that we observed throughout the project. Specifically, teachers' increased and changed knowledge and insights about assessment did not occur in a linear manner. Instead, most project participants went through marked ups and downs in their perceived knowledge and self-confidence and in their uses of alternative assessment. In some occasions teachers felt they had a clear understanding of an assessment concept or procedure, while in others they felt absolutely uncertain about their next step or about their ability to design an assessment tool. Here is an excerpt from Carolyn's letter:

> In looking through my journal/notebook, which I began at the start of the project, I stopped on the twentieth page. It was here that the entry made me stop, think, and consider. When I did this I was able to see where I was and how far I had come. Even now as I sit here and type I still feel like I have

failed, or I just don't know WHERE to begin, as I really didn't complete a design, nor did I implement anything close to a "full-blown" portfolio. You see, I wanted to be like "everybody else" when we walked in to meet on June 1, 1994. I wanted to be carrying some kind of end product to share.

Such is not the case, however, for on June 1st not only did I not have a design (just a ton of thoughts, words, attempts, papers, trials, errors), but I also couldn't admit that I didn't have something complete, so l told those I talked to that I brought the wrong bag . . .

So, let me be honest with you, as I have already to those I had not been previously. Let me focus no more on what I didn't do or don't have, but rather look in the more positive direction to show and tell you where I started, where I wept, and hopefully where I'm going.

Getting back to page 20 of my journal, I had expressed a fear of letting go of the "safety lines" of standardized practices, testing and in effect teaching. (I call them "safety lines" only because they're the standard tools and practices available and being used in my school. They're in place, they're available . . . they're junk. To use them is easier, but for me not satisfying at all.) You will see on my journey that these "safety lines" were to become ropes that would bind, gag, and pull me under. Along with me went my "crew" of 27 kids whose abilities from day one ranged from not being able to identify the sound of any of the letters of the alphabet to a few who proudly boasted that Jurassic Park (the novel, not the junior novelette!) was their favorite book.

So began the year. To make a long story short I was completely overwhelmed by the number of students but more so by the extremely wide range of abilities and by the amount of emotional, psychological, and social needs about a third of the class possessed. We began our year, this my 4th year teaching first grade. This wasn't supposed to happen. This was supposed to be an "easy" year. I had it all down. Or so l thought.

I began the way the other five first-grade teachers did. We did our initial testing (standardized, of course), put the kids into four or five ability-based groups and then tried to manage them all. By managing them I mean trying to meet with each "reading group" every day while basically keeping the others occupied with activities that all were able to do individually or in small groups independently. This, as any primary teacher would know, is an extremely difficult thing to do. In my case it was nearly impossible. It wasn't what I wanted. My heart wasn't in it. It was junk.

It was my discontent coupled with my fear that sent me fast on the track of the very long roller coaster that seems still to have no end in sight. Along the way there have been both successes and failures, trials and triumphs. One thing is for sure. Along the way in all the ups and downs I slowly and cautiously freed myself from those ropes, let go of them, and then with much happiness and force threw them off of myself and "the crew." Looking back on it now I realize it took me all year to do this.

As I learned more about authentic assessment and my mind became cluttered, my discontent grew. I took another baby step in the right direction. Not without steps backward, but nonetheless in a forward direction. (Is this possible?) I came to realize that for me to attempt authentic assessment . . . I first had to make changes in my classroom. I also had to learn to listen to and trust myself.

Well, it wasn't long before we didn't do "groups." Instead we all stuck together and did whole-group activities and projects that were usually very spontaneously spurred by an overheard conversation, a special or difficult event, or very often by a book. I specifically remember in October when we were learning the letter M we made up this class jingle about marshmallows, mashed potatoes, and a myriad of other M things that we could imagine. It was a blast. We learned it and memorized it and read all kinds of "long, hard" words. Then we sang it to Mrs. Janson's fifth grade. After we all beamed with pride and with happiness. We were learning. Better yet, we were having fun. All 28 of us were on the roller coaster ride.

So now, being the masochistic type at times, I tried to do it all. I didn't always know what to do in place of "groups," but found myself wanting to do anything but those horrible groups. Yet even still I felt almost obligated to try to get them through those horrible books with the skills in horrible isolation and the horrible tests. I felt this way because that's what their second-grade teacher would do. Wasn't I preparing these kids for second grade? So here I was trying to just get through the horrible groups real quick while also trying to manage learning centers to appeal to all ranges of abilities and interests. Then once that was out of the way I'd find us wrapped up in some neat writing project or doing something original to something old (like rewriting verses to familiar songs). The problem was that with lunch, recess, specials, and snack (as well as all the other academic areas I was hardly touching), there was little time for completion, follow-up, or thoroughness. Now, was I preparing these kids for second grade, or was I just making them feel as scattered and crazy as I was? We went up and down on our ride, happy then horrible, happy and horrible in the same day, happy . . . horrible . . . happy . . .

I just had to do something. Thus we rounded another curve on the ride and I shared my latest thoughts of how to do things with my aide. I recall speaking with her on the phone on a Sunday as I attempted to plan our upcoming week. As a matter of fact, looking into my book it was the week of April 11, 1994 that we experienced Miss Bagley the way she wanted to teach, the way her heart knew was right. They were happy. I was happy, and very, very tired, for it all happened very spontaneously. I had all the "horrible" I could take.

While Carolyn left the Hudson Valley Project at the end of the second year, her letter reveals how much change she underwent. Yet the program became too overwhelming a structure to manage that change. It did not provide her with the support she needed to reconcile or even replace the curriculum and assessments she felt she had to use with the ones she wanted to implement. I have no doubts she is on a journey to becoming a better teacher, and I wish we could have provided her with a sufficiently nurturing environment to soften the contradictions she encountered as she maneuvered the changes she attempted.

I know that many of the programmatic elements of the Hudson Valley Project are necessary for teachers to embrace authentic assessment and learner-centered pedagogy, but these are not sufficient for the kinds of changes in schools I'd like. In fact, there are inherent limitations in a program like this. One such limitation lies in the fact that only a few teachers per school or district have access to in-depth and sustained opportunities to learn about and experiment with new ways of thinking about teaching and learning. While we devoted some time to helping the project teachers share their knowledge, not all districts or professional staff welcomed the idea of teachers teaching teachers.

The number of competing demands on teaching and on schools is sometimes overwhelming to consider and I wonder if as a society we realize that an educational system cannot both reproduce society *and* transform it. At this point in time, the costs associated with creating true communities of learning appear to exceed our beliefs that the system is broken enough to deserve those communities. Yet, when I step outside the system and look at what teachers can do when they are afforded rich and supportive learning opportunities, I feel hopeful. I am eager to see more. Perhaps this is the way we ought to think—focusing on teachers one at a time, nurturing their growth, and celebrating their learning. The preceding eight chapters written by the project participants all support the belief that real change is slow, deep, and individualized.

This last teacher poem, written by Doug Young, a social studies teacher, captures the possibilities and contradictions brought about by change.

> Imagine an English class where you rewrite the last act of *Miss Saigon* and present it to the class.
> Imagine writing a newspaper that captures the stories of senior citizens who lived during the McCarthy Era.
> Imagine creating a new Constitution for the years 2000 and beyond and sharing it with some politicians.
> Imagine a computer presentation in which you demonstrate your learning for your parents.
> Imagine presenting your real-world scientific experiment in physics to a group of IBM scientists.
> Imagine creating a neighborhood walk in your city and sharing the history you found with both residents and students.
> Imagine working with people at a food bank and analyzing the nutrition value of the food for health class.
> Imagine an accounting class doing the books for a local nonprofit agency.
> Imagine students teaching what they learned in their language class with ESL students at the local elementary school for credit.
> Now imagine real hard.
> Imagine sitting down with paper and pencil and taking a multiple-choice test.

Appendix A

Protocol for the Review of
Teacher-as-Assessor Portfolios
Version 1

Portfolio developer: _____

Portfolio reviewer: _____

Grade level in which the portfolio is being used: _____

Date: _____

Please use the following key to determine the extent to which the portfolio in question addresses the criteria listed below.

not at all   1   2   3   4   5   definitively

Outcomes and indicators

_____   The portfolio includes learning outcomes to be addressed.

_____   The portfolio includes outcome indicators (what the outcomes mean to the teacher).

_____   The reader clearly understands what the outcomes and indicators mean.

_____   The portfolio describes the relationship among outcomes, indicators, and entries.

_____   The reader clearly understands the relationship among outcomes, indicators, and entries included.

Comments:

Standards and criteria

_____   The portfolio establishes clear criteria for the selection of the entries.

_____   If the portfolio is achievement related, it includes appropriate performance standards for judging the quality of the entries.

_____ The portfolio clearly distinguishes standards from expectations.

_____ If the portfolio is achievement related, it is evaluated.

_____ If the portfolio is achievement related, it includes the rubrics used to assess entries.

_____ If the portfolio is graded, the reader knows what criteria are used to assess the entries and/or the portfolio as a whole.

Comments:

Portfolio use

_____ The portfolio clearly describes the time frame that it comprises.

_____ The portfolio clearly describes the curriculum areas it addresses.

_____ The reader knows the grade level for which the portfolio is designed.

_____ The portfolio includes a thorough description of the kinds of students in the class(es) in which it is used.

_____ It is evident that the reader knows who the primary audience for the portfolio is.

_____ It is evident that the reader knows who the secondary audience(s) for the portfolio is/are.

_____ It is evident that the reader knows who owns the portfolio.

_____ It is evident that the reader knows what happens to the portfolio when it is completed.

Comments:

Scope of portfolio

_____ The portfolio appropriately documents students' achievement.

_____ The portfolio appropriately documents students' effort.

_____ The portfolio appropriately documents students' progress.

Comments:

Portfolio entries

_____ The reader understands the context surrounding each of the entries (e.g., coached, homework assignment, individual versus group work, etc.).

_____ The assignments that produce the portfolio entries are described with sufficient detail.

_____ The assignments that produce the portfolio entries are substantive.

_____ The portfolio entries are intrinsically connected to the outcomes and indicators.

_____ The portfolio clearly describes the role that the teacher, students, and/or others had in selecting portfolio entries.

_____ The portfolio allows for sufficient choice and individualization on the part of students.

_____ The portfolio entries adequately assess authentic learning.

_____ The portfolio entries are likely to sufficiently reveal students' thinking.

_____ The portfolio entries are likely to sufficiently reveal students' development.

_____ The portfolio entries require that the student reflect upon them.

_____ The portfolio entries are likely to enable students from all cultural backgrounds to demonstrate their knowledge and skills.

Comments:

Journal (and/or introductory letter to the reader)

_____ The journal clarifies the teacher's decision-making process regarding what to include in the portfolio.

_____ The journal includes sufficient evidence of the steps taken to create and refine the portfolio.

_____ The journal includes sufficient information on students' reactions to the portfolio and the required entries.

_____ The journal includes sufficient information on the demands, in terms of time and effort, imposed by the use of portfolios and other alternative assessments.

_____ The journal includes sufficient information on the extent to which the portfolio adequately captures the teachers' desired student outcomes.

_____ The journal includes sufficient information on the teacher's current assessment of the portfolio.

_____ The journal includes sufficient information on the research question that the teacher is pursuing.

Comments:

1. Overall, what are the strengths of this portfolio?

2. What are its most obvious weaknesses?

3. What are some practical suggestions for addressing these weaknesses?

4. What insights have you derived as a portfolio developer from the review process?

5. What implications does your review of this portfolio have for your own portfolio design?

Response to Peer Review and Self-Assessment

Portfolio developer: _____

1. What are the key insights you derived from your reviewer's interpretation of your portfolio?

2. What will you do to this portfolio to improve upon it?

Protocol for the Review of
Teacher-as-Assessor Portfolio

Version 2

Portfolio developer: _____

Portfolio reviewer: _____

Grade level in which the portfolio is being used: _____

Date: _____

1. Nature of learning emphasized through this portfolio (extent to which the portfolio is likely to elicit authentic learning):

2. Ways in which the portfolio is connected and supportive of the teacher's research questions:

3. Evidence of congruence among outcomes, indicators, and entries:

4. Ways in which the portfolio documents changes in the teacher's thinking about assessment and process used in its development:

5. Strengths of this portfolio:

6. Areas of concern:

7. Practical suggestions:

8. Insights about your own portfolio based on this review:

Response to Peer Review and Self-Assessment

Portfolio developer: _____

1. What are the key insights you derived from your reviewer's interpretation of your portfolio?

2. What will you do to this portfolio to improve upon its design?

Appendix B

Protocol for the Review of Students' Portfolios

Version 1

Portfolio developer: _____

Portfolio reviewer: _____

Grade: _____

Name of student: _____

Date: _____

Please use the following key to determine the extent to which the portfolio in question addresses the criteria listed below.

not at all   1   2   3   4   5   definitively

Use only one student portfolio in responding to the following questions.

_____ 1. The portfolio entries are intrinsically connected to the learner outcomes and indicators identified by the portfolio.

_____ 2. The portfolio entries provide substantive evidence of the learner outcomes and indicators identified by the portfolio.

_____ 3. The portfolio entries include sufficient information regarding the context surrounding each of the entries (e.g., coached, homework assignment, individual versus group work, etc.).

_____ 4. The student and/or teacher has clearly described why the entries have been included and how they should be interpreted.

_____ 5. The portfolio entries include substantive information regarding how the teacher assessed them.

_____ 6. The portfolio entries adequately capture the student's development in the attainment of the outcomes and indicators sought.

_____ 7. The portfolio entries sufficiently elicit authentic learning.

_____ 8. The portfolio entries adequately elicit the student's thinking regarding the processes and strategies used to complete tasks and products.

_____ 9. The student is able to individualize and customize the portfolio.

_____ 10. The assignments leading to the portfolio entries are sufficiently comprehensive and meaningful.

_____ 11. The student has clearly used the portfolio to set learning goals.

_____ 12. The student has clearly used the portfolio to monitor his/her progress in attaining learning goals.

13. What can you tell about what this student knows, is able to do, and values based upon this review? Be as detailed as possible using specific examples from the portfolios to support your assertions. Use additional space if needed.

14. To what extent are the statements that you can make about this student related to the outcomes that the measure or portfolio addresses?

   to no extent   1   2   3   4   5   to a great extent

Review three to five student portfolios before responding to the following questions.

_____ 15. The criteria for the selection of the range of students included is adequately supported.

_____ 16. The portfolio entries are likely to enable students from all cultural backgrounds to demonstrate their knowledge and skills.

_____ 17. The portfolio entries are likely to enable students with different learning needs to demonstrate their knowledge and skills.

18. What can you tell about what the teacher values and emphasizes in his/her teaching? Be as detailed as possible using specific examples from the portfolios to support your assertions. Use additional space if needed.

19. What could make these portfolios easier to understand or follow?

20. What insights have you derived as a portfolio developer from reviewing these portfolios?

21. What implications does your review of these portfolios have for your own portfolio design?

Response to Peer Review and Self-Assessment

Portfolio developer: _____

1. What are the key insights you derived from your reviewer's interpretation of your portfolio?

2. What will you do to this portfolio to improve upon it?

Protocol for the Review of Students' Portfolios
Version 2

Portfolio developer: _____

Portfolio reviewer: _____

Grade: _____

Name of student: _____

Date: _____

Respond to the following questions after reviewing one portfolio.

1. What does the portfolio tell you about:

    a. What the student knows and is able to do?

    b. What the student thinks of the portfolio?

    c. What the student reflects upon?

    d. How the student thinks?

    e. What the student has taught?

    f. What the teacher has taught?

    g. What the teacher needs to help the student improve?

2. What would you like to know about the portfolio that you do not yet know or understand?

Review three to five portfolios before responding to the following questions.

3. Is the criteria for the selection of the range of students included adequately supported?

4. How likely are the portfolio entries to enable students from different cultural backgrounds to demonstrate their knowledge and skills?

5. How likely are the portfolio entries to enable students with different learning needs to demonstrate their knowledge and skills?

6. What would make these portfolios easier for you to understand or follow?

Appendix C:
Rubric for Teacher Portfolios

The Presentation of the Teacher Portfolio

An Exemplary Portfolio

The organization of the portfolio enhances and showcases the story of the teacher's learning. All parts of the portfolio bear a clear relationship to each other and to a central purpose. The portfolio is carefully, meticulously, and attractively assembled. The writing is legible, clear, and free of grammatical error. Clearly the teacher is aware of the impact that presentation has on the reader and on the portrayal of her work.

A Developed Portfolio

The organization of the portfolio helps to tell the story of the teacher's learning. The parts of the portfolio are logically organized and help the reader to see the whole picture. The portfolio is carefully assembled. The writing is legible, clear, and free of noticeable grammatical errors. Clearly the teacher thought about her reader as she assembled and organized the portfolio.

An Emerging Portfolio

The organization of the portfolio provides some support for the story of the teacher's learning. The reader is able to make connections between some parts but has questions that interfere with complete understanding. Better or different organization of the pieces would make the big picture clearer to the reader. The writing is legible but the reader struggles with some imprecise language and notices many grammatical errors. The teacher seems to have given little thought or time to the assembly and organization of the portfolio and demonstrates little awareness of the reader.

An Undeveloped Portfolio

The organization of the portfolio takes away from the story of the teacher's learning. The reader is unable to see the connections between the parts of the portfolio. The writing is sometimes illegible or unclear and contains noticeable grammatical errors. The teacher seems to have given no thought or time to the assembly and organization of the portfolio. The reader is frustrated and angered by the teacher's apparent lack of awareness of her audience.

The Teacher-as-Learner Portfolio

An Exemplary Portfolio

Overall   The portfolio is a coherent story of the teacher as a lifelong, reflective learner engaged in the process of making meaning. When reviewing the portfolio, the reader gets to know the teacher whose work and achievements are depicted and can clearly understand her learning. The teacher is clearly aware of her audience and provides sufficient description of the context within which her work/learning has taken place.

Reader Letter, Journal Entries, and Other Reflective Pieces   The portfolio provides substantial evidence of thoughtfulness and reflectivity. The teacher's reflections reveal new insights and questions related to course content (alternative assessments, authenticity, learning theory, student reflection, rubric development, action research), to the application of new concepts to her teaching and assessment practices, and to student reactions to new practices. The reflections include an assessment of the teacher's strengths and areas for improvement as well as a description of the teacher's learning process. The teacher explicitly evaluates the degree to which assessment goals have been met and has set specific and realistic goals to extend her learning. The teacher identifies specific areas where response is needed.

A Developed Portfolio

Overall   The portfolio is a story of a teacher as a reflective learner engaged in the process of making meaning. When reviewing the portfolio, the reader begins to get to know the teacher whose work and achievements are depicted and can see that significant learning has taken place. The teacher writes more for herself than for the audience. Therefore, the context of the learning is sometimes unclear to the reader.

Dear Reader Letter, Journal Entries, and Other Reflective Pieces   The portfolio provides clear evidence of thoughtfulness and reflectivity. The teacher's reflections reveal new insights and questions related to course content (alternative assessments, authenticity, learning theory, student reflection, rubric development, action research), to the application of new concepts to her teaching and assessment practices, and to student reactions to new practices. The teacher has reflected on her strengths and weaknesses and has begun to describe her learning process and to set specific goals for the future.

An Emerging Portfolio

Overall   The portfolio is becoming a story of the teacher as a reflective learner. When reviewing the portfolio, the reader learns about the teacher's work and achievements but sees snapshots rather than an entire story. The reader can see that learning has taken place but cannot see how.

Dear Reader Letter, Journal Entries, and Other Reflective Pieces   The
portfolio reveals some evidence of thoughtfulness and reflectivity. The
teacher's reflections center around course content (alternative assessments,
authenticity, learning theory, student reflection, rubric development, action research) and application to her own teaching practice. It is clear to the reader
where the teacher is succeeding and where she is struggling, though the
teacher hasn't explicitly stated her awareness of the areas. The reader is able
to identify areas for specific feedback.

An Undeveloped Portfolio

Overall   The portfolio includes some story elements but doesn't yet tell a
story of the teacher as a reflective learner. The reader sees the teacher's products but cannot see the process and thinking behind them.

Dear Reader Letter, Journal Entries, and Other Reflective Pieces   There
is little evidence of thoughtfulness or reflectivity in the portfolio. The reflective pieces, if included, offer little or no information about what the teacher
does and little or no view of the teacher behind the work. The reader is unable
to provide feedback because there is so little information about the teacher's
thinking and learning process.

The Teacher-as-Curriculum-and-Assessment-Developer Portfolio

An Exemplary Portfolio

Overall   The portfolio tells the story of the teacher whose goal is to make instruction and assessment practices one and the same, embedded in a curriculum
designed around students' outcomes of great significance. The portfolio reveals
the teacher's outstanding ability to apply curriculum- and assessment-related
concepts and skills to the development of lessons, activities, and assessments
that target clearly defined outcomes. The teacher has provided all drafts of assessments, allowing the reader to see changes and improvements made to apply
design principles and to align curriculum, instruction, and assessment.

Context   The portfolio provides a thorough and clear picture of the teacher's
curriculum, including the concepts, themes, skills, and assessments. The connections between these elements are obvious and clear. The outcomes around which
the curriculum is designed are significant, precisely stated in terms of student
learning, and further described with specific and observable indicators.

Assessment Plan (Two or Three New Assessments or Student Portfolio)
The plan meshes beautifully with the teacher's instruction. The assessments
are learning opportunities and vice versa. The descriptions of the assessments

are thorough and provide all the needed context, including content area focus, targeted outcomes with indicators, intended purpose, and detailed descriptions of activities that precede and follow the assessments. The reader completely understands how the assessments fit into the curriculum and the roles that teachers, students, parents, and others play in their use. Finally, the amount of time and effort imposed by the assessments is clearly stated.

Portfolio Design   The portfolio design is clearly student driven and owned. It has a real purpose and audience and documents student achievement, effort, and growth toward significant and clearly stated outcomes. The reader clearly sees how the portfolio fits into the curriculum and the roles of teachers, students, and others in its development. There is a clear description of how students select and reflect upon their work. The teacher evaluates the portfolio using clearly defined and shared performance criteria, which students use in the evaluation process.

Description of Assessments   The assessments are truly authentic. They are curriculum-embedded, substantive, and integrative tasks that require students to build upon prior knowledge, apply knowledge and skills from one or more content areas, express conclusions through elaborate communications, use metacognitive strategies, rethink, and revise. The assessments are valued by audiences outside of school, have a real purpose, and are sufficiently flexible to allow all students choice and opportunity for success. They are relevant to students' lives and sensitive to different needs and cultural backgrounds.

The assessments include measures that guide student reflection on both products and processes that may take the form of specific questions, checklists, or rubrics. Reflections and prompts show the teacher's understanding of the need to accommodate the various developmental levels and learning styles. The teacher has included student work with clear explanations about how the assessments work with different students. The teacher has described the degree to which the target students capture the diversity of the classroom, allowing the reader to draw conclusions about the value of the assessment for wide ranges in student ability and knowledge.

Standards of Performance   The standards of performance for the assessment tasks are clear to everyone. They were jointly identified and articulated by teacher and students in rubrics, scoring criteria, and/or exemplars. They effectively guide students in evaluating their work and setting goals for improvement. The rubric design perfectly matches the assessment. Students are able to find the targeted skills at every level on the rubric and can use the levels described to build upon their learning and set specific goals. The lower levels outnumber the higher levels, making the rubric an excellent scaffolding and instructional tool. The top level is above the expected standard—even the highest achiever is challenged to improve. In addition, the rubric includes sample evidence for each level, which the students helped to identify and evaluate.

A Developed Portfolio

Overall   The portfolio tells the story of the teacher as an assessor whose goal is to align explicit instruction and assessment practices and embed them in a curriculum designed around outcomes. The portfolio reveals the teacher's ability to apply curriculum- and assessment-related concepts and skills to the development of lessons, activities, and assessments that target clearly defined outcomes. The teacher has provided drafts of assessments, allowing the reader to see changes and improvements the teacher has made in an effort to apply design principles and align curriculum, instruction, and assessment.

Context   The portfolio provides a clear picture of the teacher's curriculum. The reader can see the concepts, themes, skills, and assessments that make up the curriculum. The connections between these elements are clear to the reader. The outcomes around which the curriculum is designed are important, are stated in terms of student learning, and are further described with specific and observable indicators.

Assessment Plan (Two or Three New Assessments or Student Portfolio)
The teacher's assessment plan is congruent and meshes with her instruction. Many of the assessments are embedded into the curriculum and are supportive of learning. The descriptions of the assessments include a description of the context, including the content area focus, the outcomes targeted, the identification of the indicators that support the outcomes, and the intended purpose of the assessments. The reader is able to see how the assessments fit into the curriculum and the roles that teachers, students, parents, and others play in their use. Finally, the reader can estimate the amount of time and effort imposed by the assessment.

Portfolio Design   The portfolio design is both teacher and student driven with both parties sharing ownership. It documents student achievement, effort, and growth toward significant and clearly stated outcomes. The reader clearly sees how the portfolio fits into the curriculum and the roles that teacher and students play in its development. The teacher has described the selection process and includes student guidelines for selection and reflection. The reader is unsure of how the portfolio is evaluated or how it relates to the report card.

Description of Assessments   The assessments described include authentic and performance assessments. They are curriculum embedded, substantive, and integrative tasks that require students to build upon prior knowledge, apply knowledge and skills from one or more content areas, express conclusions through communications, and use metacognitive strategies. The assessments could be improved by providing an audience outside of school or by providing a real purpose. The assessments allow some flexibility in terms of time and measures to allow students some choice and opportunity for success. They are relevant to students' lives and sensitive to different needs and cultural backgrounds.

The assessments include measures that guide student reflection and self-assessment of either products or processes that may take the form of specific questions, checklists, or rubrics. The teacher has included sample student work resulting from the assessment.

Standards of Performance   The standards of performance for the assessment tasks are clear to everyone. The teacher identified and articulated them with some student participation. The rubric design fits the assessment and the targeted skills appear at all levels on the rubric. The descriptions effectively distinguish between levels of performance. Students can use the levels described to build upon their learning and to set specific goals. The rubric may need one or more of the following: (1) more lower levels, (2) a top level that is above the expected standard so that even the highest achiever is challenged to improve, and (3) sample evidence for each level.

An Emerging Portfolio

Overall   The portfolio tells the story of the teacher as an assessor whose goal is to align her instruction and assessment practices and embed them in a curriculum designed around important outcomes for students rather than content objectives. The portfolio clearly reveals the teacher's ability to apply some curriculum- and assessment-related concepts and skills to the development of lessons, activities, and assessments.

Context   The portfolio provides a picture of the teacher's curriculum. The reader is able to see the concepts and themes, but the skills and assessments connected to those concepts and themes aren't as clear. The outcomes around which the teacher is working are important and are, for the most part, stated in terms of student learning. The reader has difficulty seeing the relationship between the outcomes and the teacher's curriculum. The language of the outcomes could be improved by removing references to specific content areas and could be made more clear with specific and observable indicators.

Assessment Plan (Two or Three New Assessments or Student Portfolio)
The teacher's assessment plan fits in some ways with her instruction. There is evidence that the teacher is aligning assessment and instruction, as some of the assessments are learning opportunities. The content area focus of the assessments is clear to the reader. The reader is unsure of the purpose of the assessment and which outcomes the assessment is intended to target. The reader is able to see how the assessments fit into the curriculum but is unsure of the roles that teachers, students, parents, and others play in their use.

Portfolio Design   The portfolio design is mostly teacher driven, and the teacher seems to own more of the portfolio than the student does. The portfolio has a real purpose for the teacher, and a limited audience. It documents student achievement toward stated outcomes but can be improved by incorporating the documentation of growth and effort. The reader sees how the portfolio fits into the curriculum, but the role that the student plays in the selection of pieces and the development of the portfolio is limited or unclear. The reader is unsure of how the portfolio is evaluated or how it contributes to the report card.

Description of Assessments   The assessments described are related to the curriculum. It is difficult to determine their substantiveness and rigor. They require that students build upon prior knowledge and apply knowledge and skills from one or two content areas. The assessments could be improved by doing one or more of the following: (1) integrating other content areas; (2) requiring students to do more elaborate communicating; (3) requiring students to use metacognitive strategies; (4) providing an audience outside of school; or (5) providing a real purpose. The assessments require a predefined mode of representation and are flexible in that students can choose from a list of options.

The assessments may be accompanied by reflective questions that are peripherally related to the assessments. The teacher has included student work derived from the assessments but information is missing about how these relate to one another. The reader needs more information about the students in order to make any inferences about the degree to which they capture the diversity of the classroom or to draw any conclusions about the value of the assessment for wide ranges in student ability and knowledge.

Standards of Performance   The standards of performance have been partially identified by the teacher and students in checklists or scoring rubrics that help students evaluate their work as a whole. While the targeted skills appear at most levels on the rubric, the descriptions have only begun to distinguish between levels of performance. The students can use the levels described to identify where they are on the rubric but may need more information to use the rubric as a scaffolding tool that will allow them to build upon their learning and set specific goals. The rubric may be improved by doing several of the following: (1) further describing the levels to distinguish them from each other; (2) incorporating more lower levels; (3) making the top level above the expected standard so that even the highest achiever is challenged to improve; and (4) including sample evidence for each level.

An Undeveloped Portfolio

Overall   The portfolio provides little or no view of the teacher as an assessor working toward integrating curriculum, instruction, and assessment. The portfolio reveals the teacher's ability to teach to the curriculum and to develop lessons and activities. The teacher's assessments are summative only and are designed to measure learning.

Context   The portfolio provides a picture of the teacher's curriculum. The reader is able to see the concepts and themes that make up the curriculum but is unable to see the skills and assessments connected to those concepts and themes. The outcomes around which the teacher is working are curriculum-focused rather than student-centered or are not stated. The reader is unable to tell what the teacher wants her students to know or be able to do outside of specific content-related objectives.

Assessment Plan (Two or Three New Assessments or Student Portfolio) The teacher's assessment plan is separate from her instruction. There is little or no evidence that the teacher is aligning assessment and instruction, as most assessments come after lessons and activities and are summative in nature. The content area focus and purpose of the assessments are unclear.

Portfolio Design   The portfolio design is not clear to the reader. The student role is not defined or the student has little or no role in the selection of pieces for the portfolio. The purpose of the portfolio is unclear, as is the intended audience. The portfolio seems to be a random collection of student work—the reader is unsure of what the portfolio is intended to document, and it is unclear how the portfolio fits into the classroom or is used by the teacher and students.

Description of Assessments   The assessments described are curriculum embedded and require that students recall or recognize concepts. The assessments appear to have little relevance to students' lives.

The assessments allow for little or no student reflection. The teacher is the only one who evaluates and assesses the students' work. Finally, the reader is unable to see how the assessments work with students since the teacher has not included sample student work.

Standards of Performance   The standards of performance for the assessment tasks are not evident or have been partially articulated by the teacher. Students are unable to use performance criteria to evaluate themselves or improve upon their performance.

The Teacher-as-Researcher Portfolio

An Exemplary Portfolio

Overall   The portfolio tells the story of the teacher-as-researcher in the process of looking for answers to questions that are at the heart of her thinking. The teacher's action research extends naturally from her work and drives her thinking. The reader gets a clear picture of a teacher who is always wearing the "hat" of a researcher—observing, noting, and thinking about what happens and why.

Action Research   The teacher's assessment work and reflections clearly connect to the teacher's stated research question(s). The designed research plan is sound and methods of collection fit snugly into the teacher's assessment design. The research is an integral and natural part of the teacher's work. The data collected is clearly presented, accurately summarized, and thoroughly analyzed. The reader can only agree with the conclusions drawn as the evidence provided is inarguable and compelling. New questions naturally emerge for the research and provide direction for further study. The teacher is compelled to continue the quest for answers to these new questions and has clearly defined a plan for continued research efforts.

A Developed Portfolio

Overall   The portfolio tells the story of the teacher-as-researcher in the process of looking for answers to specific questions. The teacher's research extends naturally from her work. The reader gets a clear picture of a teacher who often wears the "hat" of a researcher—observing, noting, and thinking about what happens and why.

Action Research   The teacher's assessment work and reflections clearly connect to the teacher's stated research question(s). The research plan is sound and methods of collection fit into the teacher's assessment design. The research is an integral and natural part of the teacher's work. The data collected by the teacher is clearly presented and the teacher has begun to draw answers to her questions from it. The reader understands the conclusions drawn and can see evidence in the portfolio to support the conclusions. The teacher has identified new research questions for further study.

An Emerging Portfolio

Overall   The portfolio begins to tell a story of the teacher-as-researcher who is looking for answers to specific research questions related to her work. The reader gets a picture of a teacher who is just learning to wear the "hat" of a researcher—learning to act and think as a researcher.

Action Research   The teacher's research question is stated, but the reader is not sure how the research connects to the teacher's assessment work. The teacher's reflections include discussion of the action research but do not discuss it in light of the other work done. The research work seems to stand apart from the teacher's assessment work. The reader can envision how the teacher might incorporate the research more effectively and can see data embedded in the work included in the portfolio. The teacher's next steps are to reflect on the research work done and clarify the connections to the assessment work.

An Undeveloped Portfolio

Overall   The portfolio includes mention of action research but doesn't tell a story of a teacher-as-researcher. The reader gets a picture of a teacher who has yet to wear the "hat" of a researcher.

Action Research   There is no stated research questions or, if there is, the reader can find no evidence that the teacher is actively doing research connected to the question(s). The teacher's reflections do not mention the research. The reader is unable to see connections between the stated research question(s) and the assessment work included in the portfolio.

The Teacher-as-Staff-Developer Portfolio

An Exemplary Portfolio

Overall   The portfolio tells the story of a teacher who has clearly defined her areas of expertise and who has outstanding ability to share that expertise. By leading workshops, facilitating collegial circles, coaching peers, and writing articles for publication, the teacher is contributing to the collective knowledge of teachers.

Description of Activities   The teacher's portfolio includes thorough descriptions of professional development activities that build on the teacher's expertise. The context is described and consistent with the teacher's planned activities. The programs accommodate the various levels of experience of the audience and are based on sound learning theory and an understanding of conditions that support adult learning. The presentation serves as a model for good staff development.

Supporting Resources   The materials used by the teacher are clear, precise, professional, and attractive. The teacher has consistently sought feedback from participants and included the feedback in the portfolio.

Reflection and Analysis   The teacher has reflected on her own learning as a staff developer and specifically discusses strengths and areas for improvement. She has summarized the feedback and has used it to inform future plans. Finally, the teacher has set clear, specific goals for further staff development activities and documentation of expertise.

A Developed Portfolio

Overall   The portfolio tells the story of a teacher who has taken on the role of staff developer and is sharing knowledge and experiences with colleagues. By leading workshops, facilitating collegial circles, and coaching peers, the teacher is facilitating the learning of teachers in her community.

Description of Activities   The teacher's portfolio includes descriptions of activities. The context is described and is consistent with the teacher's plans. The activities accommodate the various levels of experience that the audience brings and incorporate good teaching practices.

Supporting Resources   The materials used by the teacher are clear and neat. The teacher has sought feedback from participants and has included the feedback in the portfolio.

Reflection and Analysis   The teacher has reflected on her own learning as a staff developer and has identified strengths and areas for improvement.

An Emerging Portfolio

Overall   The portfolio tells the story of a teacher who has begun to take on the role of staff developer by either leading a workshop, facilitating a collegial circle, or coaching peers. The teacher is recognized as someone willing to share knowledge and experiences.

Description of Activities   The teacher's portfolio includes descriptions of activities.

Supporting Resources   The materials used by the teacher in facilitating the various staff development activities are clear and neat.

Reflection and Analysis   The teacher has reflected on her activities and has identified ways to improve them.

An Undeveloped Portfolio

Overall   The portfolio tells the story of a teacher who is informally sharing knowledge and experiences with colleagues. The teacher is becoming recognized in her community as someone who is willing to share knowledge and experiences.

Description of Activities   The teacher's informal sharing activities are mentioned briefly within the context of her portfolio.

Supporting Resources   The materials used by the teachers are not organized in ways that make it possible for the reader to see how they are used.

Reflection and Analysis   The teacher has reflected on her activities in very general ways and has not identified ways to improve them.

Appendix D: Teacher Simulation

Teacher Guidelines

Context

Pioneer Central School District is a small, suburban district. It has two buildings (a pre-K to sixth-grade building) and a seventh- to twelfth-grade building). It has about 115 teachers and about 1,100 students. Two years ago, a
committee comprised of six teachers, four administrators, and three parents
generated six exit outcomes, two of which are *effective communication* and
critical thinking. After a period of review by staff and community members,
the board of education decided to ratify the outcomes. They also proposed
that the district explore the use of portfolios as a means for documenting students' attainment of these outcomes. The superintendent and top administrative staff have formed an assessment committee comprised of two teachers
from each grade level and the school principals from the two buildings.

Audience

Twenty of the twenty-four teachers and one of the two principals has little if
any prior knowledge about alternative assessment. The other principal has recently moved to the area from Kentucky, and he is calling for a K–12 standardized portfolio in communication and critical thinking. The remaining
four teachers have a working understanding of alternative assessment, and
three of them have developed and used classroom-based portfolios.

Goal

You will make a *twenty-minute* presentation to the committee. Your primary
objective is to persuade the committee members of the value of teacher-
generated portfolios. Since this committee is empowered to recommend
strategies for implementing assessment-related changes, you need to provide
committee members with a working understanding of what it takes for teachers to design and implement classroom-based portfolios. You will use your
experience designing and using portfolios as the *primary* resource for your
presentation. Through your "story" you will try to educate your audience
about different assessment-related components (e.g., self-reflection, rubrics,
exemplars, etc.).

Before our next session:

1. Review all the different drafts you have produced of your design and identify the major changes your design has gone through.

2. Review your logs, journals, and letters to the reader. Identify what you think are key "excerpts" that depict what you have learned about alternative assessment, about teaching, about students, or about yourself.

3. Create a handout of no more than five pages that "captures" your design and your learning about assessment. These may include rubrics, student samples, letters to readers, definitions, and self-reflective exercises. Make sure that the "excerpts" you have identified are included in this handout. Make four copies of your handout.

Your presentation may include *some or all* of the following components:

1. A brief description of the grade level and subject you teach

2. Your student population

3. The outcomes that guide your design

4. The role that students play in selecting and evaluating their work

5. The process for selecting portfolio materials

6. Your use of rubrics or standards

7. What you have learned about your students and about assessment

8. The changes you have made since you began your design

9. What you think would be lost if teachers were not able to design their own portfolios

10. The kind of training and support teachers need to do what you have done

Audience Roles and Evaluation Guidelines

Roles

Teacher with No Knowledge of Assessment   You are a very traditional teacher who has taught for fifteen years. You basically like students and teaching but do not like to work too hard. You are the kind of person who does not seek opportunities for professional growth, but you will consider doing things differently if you are persuaded. You do not know anything about alternative assessment, and you have heard that portfolios take a lot of time.

Teacher with Prior Exposure to Authentic Assessment and Portfolios
You are a relatively new teacher who has taken one or two workshops on authentic assessment and portfolios. Based on these workshops you tried creating a portfolio for your students but you were overwhelmed by the process and logistics so you gave it up.

Principal   You are a "hands-on" type of person. You see your job as that of leading the way for teachers. You value efficiency and order. Your desk is neatly ordered and you follow your list of "to dos" sequentially. While working in Kentucky for three years you learned about the Kentucky assessment system, and all your knowledge of portfolio assessment is derived from that experience. You like the idea of producing some kind of manual with guidelines and assessment forms for every teacher in the district. You think that the assessment committee could and should produce this manual and that every teacher should be expected to use it without much difficulty.

Evaluation Guidelines

Throughout the presentation, you will act in ways that are consistent with your role. You will then evaluate the merits of the presentation in terms of achieving its goal. In your evaluation, be very specific and consider the following questions:

Role: _____

1. What aspects of the presentation were effective in terms of persuading you of the value of teacher-developed portfolios?

2. What did you learn about alternative assessment in general and about portfolios in particular?

3. What, if anything, was redundant or unnecessary?

4. What would you have liked to see or hear more of?

Index